Young Believer Instant Message

Dear Alexandra

Praying that you'll come to Know Jesus more as you read about Him and His word.

With love,
Michelle,
Stage 3 at FCC.

Instant Messages
for Real Life

"For I Know the plans I have for you
says the Lord,
plans to prosper you and not to harm you,
plans to give you hope and a future."
-Jeremiah 29 v11

Tyndale House Publishers, Inc.
Wheaton, IL

Instant Messages for Real Life

Young Believer™ INSTANT MESSAGE

Visit Tyndale's exciting Web site at www.tyndale.com

Visit the Young Believer Web site at www.youngbeliever.com

Questions, notes, and Scripture selection primarily by Jonathan Gray

Contributing writers: Rhonda O'Brien and Shawn A. Harrison

General Editors: V. Gilbert Beers and Ronald A. Beers

ISBN 1-4143-0042-5

Printed in the United States of America

08 07 06 05 04
5 4 3 2 1

○○○ Acceptance ○○○

How can I earn God's acceptance?

Romans 3:27
Can we boast, then, that we have done anything to be accepted by God? No, because our acquittal is not based on our good deeds. It is based on our faith.

Colossians 2:6
And now, just as you accepted Christ Jesus as your Lord, you must continue to live in obedience to him.

○○○ We cannot earn God's acceptance. But his acceptance is available for free to you and to everyone. All we need to do is believe that his Son, Jesus, died for our sins so that we can be free to enjoy eternal life with him. When we accept his forgiveness and ask him to be the Lord of our life, he completely accepts us into his presence.

How do we learn to accept those who are different from us?

Matthew 9:11-12
"Why does your teacher eat with such scum?" they asked his disciples. . . . Jesus replied, "Healthy people don't need a doctor—sick people do."

○○○ Every person is a unique creation of God, loved by God. If God loves everyone, shouldn't we?

What if a person has committed a terrible sin? Should we still accept him or her?

Romans 8:39
Nothing . . . will ever be able to separate us from the love of God that is revealed in Christ Jesus our Lord.

Nothing we do can separate us from God's love. In the same way, we should always love others. This does not mean that we accept their sinful actions, but we love and accept people. God created them, and that makes them special.

Is there anything we should never accept?

2 Chronicles 34:4
He saw to it that the altars for the images of Baal and their incense altars were torn down.

We must not accept sin. Sin is our enemy, seeking to destroy us. If we let any sin dwell in our heart without asking for God's forgiveness, it will begin to spread like a disease, affecting all we think and do.

PROMISE FROM GOD:

Romans 15:7
Accept each other just as Christ has accepted you; then God will be glorified.

Advice

Why do I need advice from others? I know what I'm doing.

Proverbs 12:15
Fools think they need no advice, but the wise listen to others.

Part of growing up means recognizing our own faults. Foolishness is thinking we can do everything ourselves, without help from others.

Where do I look for good advice?

Genesis 6:9
Noah was a righteous man. . . . He consistently followed God's will and enjoyed a close relationship with him.

Titus 1:15
Everything is pure to those whose hearts are pure.

••• Seek advice from people who obey God and are honest and trustworthy. They can be counted on to give you advice that comes from God's Word.

How do I know whether someone's advice is good?

Matthew 7:16
You can detect them by the way they act, just as you can identify a tree by its fruit.

2 John 1:9
If you wander beyond the teaching of Christ, you will not have fellowship with God.

••• To know whether to listen to someone's advice, check it against the truth of God's Word. If it doesn't agree with the Bible, then it is bad advice.

How do I give good advice to others?

Philippians 4:8
Fix your thoughts on what is true and honorable and right. Think about things that are pure and lovely and admirable. Think about things that are excellent and worthy of praise.

••• When giving advice to others, follow what the Bible says. Pray about what you want to say, and have the other person's best interests in mind. Words are like medicine; they should be measured with care. An overdose may do more harm than good.

What happens when I follow good advice?

Psalm 1:1
Oh, the joys of those who do not follow the advice of the wicked, or stand around with sinners, or join in with scoffers.

Following evil advice leads to sorrow and disaster and robs us of joy and satisfaction. Godly advice leads to good results, giving us more joy.

PROMISE FROM GOD:

Psalm 32:8
I will guide you along the best pathway for your life. I will advise you and watch over you.

Anger

Why do we usually get angry?

Numbers 22:29
"Because you have made me look like a fool!" Balaam shouted.

We get angry when our pride is hurt.

Genesis 4:4-5
The Lord accepted Abel and his offering, but he did not accept Cain and his offering. This made Cain very angry and dejected.

We get angry when someone else gets more praise or attention than we do.

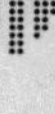

2 Chronicles 26:18-19
"Get out of the sanctuary, for you have sinned." Uzziah was furious and refused to set down the incense burner he was holding.

Esther 3:2, 5
Mordecai refused to bow down or show [Haman] respect. . . . [Haman] was filled with rage.

••• We get angry when we don't get our way.

1 Samuel 18:8
This made Saul very angry. "What's this?" he said. "They credit David with ten thousands and me with only thousands."

••• We get angry when we become jealous of what others have or what they have done.

1 Kings 22:18, 27
"Didn't I tell you?" the king of Israel said. . . . "He never prophesies anything but bad news for me. . . . Put this man in prison, and feed him nothing but bread and water."

••• We get angry when we are caught and punished for doing something wrong.

When is it okay to be angry?

John 2:15-16
[Jesus] drove out the sheep and oxen, scattered the money changers' coins . . . and . . . told them, "Get these things out of here. Don't turn my Father's house into a marketplace!"

Numbers 25:11
Phinehas . . . has turned my anger away from the Israelites by displaying passionate zeal among them on my behalf.

••• Anger at sin is okay.

When we are angry, what shouldn't we do?

James 3:5
The tongue is a small thing, but what enormous damage it can do.

••• Be careful what you say when you are angry. You might say something you'll regret.

1 Samuel 19:9-10
As David played his harp for the king, Saul hurled his spear at David in an attempt to kill him.

••• Avoid acting on impulse in the heat of anger. You are bound to do something you will regret.

We all get angry at times, so what should we do about it?

Ephesians 4:26-27
Don't sin by letting anger gain control over you. Don't let the sun go down while you are still angry, for anger gives a mighty foothold to the Devil.

••• Anger is like a wild skunk in the house. We shouldn't feed it to encourage it to stay. And we should try to get rid of it as soon as possible.

PROMISE FROM GOD:

Psalm 103:8
The Lord is merciful and gracious; he is slow to get angry and full of unfailing love.

◦◦◦ Appearance ◦◦◦

Can I trust people based on their appearance?

Isaiah 53:3
He was despised and rejected—a man of sorrows, acquainted with bitterest grief. We turned our backs on him and looked the other way when he went by. He was despised, and we did not care.

Matthew 23:28
You try to look like upright people outwardly, but inside your hearts are filled with hypocrisy and lawlessness.

◦◦◦ Appearances can often be misleading. Jesus came to earth as a man and was rejected and murdered by his own people. Be careful not to judge people based on how they look.

How important is it to maintain a good appearance?

Colossians 3:17
Whatever you do or say, let it be as a representative of the Lord Jesus, all the while giving thanks through him to God the Father.

Matthew 7:20
Yes, the way to identify a tree or a person is by the kind of fruit that is produced.

◦◦◦ As representatives of Christ, how we act around others is important, but even more important is the condition of our heart that leads to those actions.

PROMISE FROM GOD:

1 Samuel 16:7
The Lord looks at a person's thoughts and intentions.

Astrology

Is astrology wrong?

Exodus 20:3
Do not worship any other gods besides me.

2 Kings 21:6
Manasseh even sacrificed his own son in the fire. He practiced sorcery and divination, and he consulted with mediums and psychics. He did much that was evil in the Lord's sight, arousing his anger.

Occult practices, including astrology, involve worshipping other gods, which makes God very angry.

Can astrology give us direction?

Genesis 1:16-17
God made two great lights, the sun and the moon, to shine down upon the earth. . . . He also made the stars. God set these lights in the heavens to light the earth.

Don't seek advice from the stars, but from God, the Creator of the stars. Only he can give you direction for your life, because he created you, too.

PROMISE FROM GOD:

Isaiah 58:11
The Lord will guide you continually.

Backsliding

What do I do when I've fallen away from God?

Amos 5:4
This is what the Lord says to the family of Israel: "Come back to me and live!"

Romans 3:23-24
All have sinned; all fall short of God's glorious standard. Yet now God in his gracious kindness declares us not guilty. He has done this through Christ Jesus, who has freed us by taking away our sins.

Because of our sinful nature, there are times when we all fall away from God. Yet once we've identified and confessed our sin, God is faithful to forgive us. There is no sin so great that we cannot come back to God.

How can I avoid backsliding?

Ezekiel 37:23
They will stop polluting themselves with their detestable idols and other sins, for I will save them from their sinful backsliding. I will cleanse them. Then they will truly be my people, and I will be their God.

1 Peter 1:14
Obey God because you are his children. Don't slip back into your old ways of doing evil; you didn't know any better then.

Matthew 26:41
Keep alert and pray. Otherwise temptation will overpower you. For though the spirit is willing enough, the body is weak!

1 Corinthians 10:13
Remember that the temptations that come into your life are no different from what others experience. And God is faithful. He will keep the temptation from becoming so strong that you can't stand up against it. When you are tempted, he will show you a way out so that you will not give in to it.

Obedience to God's Word, prayer, and being alert to temptation help us stay away from backsliding.

Are others affected when I backslide?

Matthew 18:7
How terrible it will be for anyone who causes others to sin. Temptation to do wrong is inevitable, but how terrible it will be for the person who does the tempting.

When we sin, it almost always affects someone else too. This is why we must ask God to help us overcome the temptation to sin.

PROMISE FROM GOD:

Psalm 32:5
Finally, I confessed all my sins to you. . . . And you forgave me!

Beauty

What does God consider beautiful?

1 Peter 3:4
You should be known for the beauty that comes from within, the unfading beauty of a gentle and quiet spirit, which is so precious to God.

●●● The more we follow God's ways and show his love to others, the more his beauty shines through us. What could be more beautiful than having God's love in us?

How important to God is my outward appearance?

Proverbs 31:30
Charm is deceptive, and beauty does not last; but a woman who fears the Lord will be greatly praised.

1 Samuel 16:7
People judge by outward appearance, but the Lord looks at a person's thoughts and intentions.

James 1:23
If you just listen and don't obey, it is like looking at your face in a mirror but doing nothing to improve your appearance.

●●● Outward beauty only shows what we look like. Inner beauty is about who we are. Following God's ways causes us to reflect his beauty from the inside out.

How can my words be beautiful?

Proverbs 15:26
The Lord despises the thoughts of the wicked, but he delights in pure words.

Proverbs 25:11
Timely advice is as lovely as golden apples in a silver basket.

●●● Beautiful words come from godly thoughts and character.

How can my worship be beautiful?

Psalm 33:1
Let the godly sing with joy to the Lord, for it is fitting to praise him.

••• Beautiful worship is a result of a beautiful relationship with God.

PROMISE FROM GOD:

Proverbs 19:22
Loyalty makes a person attractive.

••• *Behavior* •••

What does God expect in my behavior?

1 Timothy 4:12
Don't let anyone think less of you because you are young. Be an example to all believers in what you teach, in the way you live, in your love, your faith, and your purity.

••• God wants each of us to be an example of Christ to others.

Romans 12:2
Don't copy the behavior and customs of this world, but let God transform you into a new person by changing the way you think.

••• God expects to transform our behavior to please him.

Romans 13:13
We should be decent and true in everything we do, so that everyone can approve of our behavior. Don't participate in wild parties and getting drunk, or in adultery and immoral living, or in fighting and jealousy.

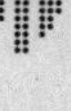

God expects us to live by his standards, which will please others and bring glory to God.

How does my behavior affect others?

1 Samuel 20:34
Jonathan left the table . . . and refused to eat all that day, for he was crushed by his father's shameful behavior toward David.

The selfishness of poor behavior often hurts the people we love the most.

Why is godly behavior so important?

Matthew 5:16
Let your good deeds shine out for all to see, so that everyone will praise your heavenly Father.

Ephesians 4:32
Be kind to each other, tenderhearted, forgiving one another, just as God through Christ has forgiven you.

Titus 2:12
We are instructed to turn from godless living and sinful pleasures. We should live in this evil world with self-control, right conduct, and devotion to God.

When people see godly behavior in us, they'll want to know what makes us different. Then we have a great opportunity to tell them that it's God's love in us!

PROMISE FROM GOD:

Luke 11:28
Even more blessed are all who hear the word of God and put it into practice.

Belief

Why should I have belief in God?

Isaiah 25:9
This is the Lord, in whom we trusted. Let us rejoice in the salvation he brings!

John 5:24
I assure you, those who listen to my message and believe in God who sent me have eternal life.

Belief is the only way to get to heaven. It is the only doorway to eternal life. If God created eternity, then we can get there only through God.

Hebrews 11:1
What is faith? It is the confident assurance that what we hope for is going to happen.

Belief gives us hope.

How does belief in God affect my relationship with him? How does it change the way I live?

Genesis 15:6
Abram believed the Lord, and the Lord declared him righteous because of his faith.

Romans 3:24-25
Now God in his gracious kindness declares us not guilty. . . . We are made right with God when we believe that Jesus shed his blood, sacrificing his life for us.

Sin breaks our relationship with God because it's rebellion against him. A holy God cannot live with unholy

people. But when we accept Jesus as Savior and ask him to forgive our sins, this simple act of belief makes us righteous in God's sight.

Isaiah 26:3
You will keep in perfect peace all who trust in you.

●●● Belief in God brings peace of mind and heart because we know that we belong to him and that one day all pain and suffering will end.

Romans 8:5
Those who are controlled by the Holy Spirit think about things that please the Spirit.

1 Corinthians 12:1
I will write about the special abilities the Holy Spirit gives to each of us.

●●● Belief is inviting God's Holy Spirit to live within us. He gives us God's power to live in a totally new way. If God himself is living within us, our life should show it.

When I'm struggling and having doubts, does it mean I don't believe?

2 Peter 1:4-5
He has given us all of his rich and wonderful promises. . . . So make every effort to apply the benefits of these promises to your life.

Genesis 15:8
Abram replied, "O Sovereign Lord, how can I be sure that you will give it to me?"

Matthew 11:2-3
John the Baptist . . . sent his disciples to ask Jesus, "Are you really the Messiah we've been waiting for?"

Many people in the Bible whom we consider to be "pillars of faith" had moments of doubt. The key is to never stop believing and to always ask if, over time, our life has been moving closer to or farther away from God. Even during moments of doubt, we must put the effort into letting our faith grow.

PROMISE FROM GOD:

Acts 16:31
Believe on the Lord Jesus and you will be saved, along with your entire household.

Bible

How can a book written so long ago be important for me today?

Hebrews 4:12
The Word of God is full of living power. It is sharper than the sharpest knife, cutting deep into our innermost thoughts and desires. It exposes us for what we really are.

2 Timothy 3:16-17
All Scripture is inspired by God and is useful to teach us what is true and to make us realize what is wrong in our lives. It straightens us out and teaches us to do what is right. It is God's way of preparing us in every way, fully equipped for every good thing God wants us to do.

Isaiah 40:8
The grass withers, and the flowers fade, but the word of our God stands forever.

••• Even though it was written long ago, the Bible is God's Word to us today, and it tells us everything we need to know to live right.

Why is it important to memorize Bible verses?

Deuteronomy 30:14
The message is very close at hand; it is on your lips and in your heart so that you can obey it.

Psalm 37:31
They fill their hearts with God's law, so they will never slip from his path.

Psalm 119:11
I have hidden your word in my heart, that I might not sin against you.

••• What you fill your heart and mind with is what you become. Memorizing Scripture helps you call God's life-changing words to mind at any time.

How can the Bible give me guidance?

Psalm 73:23-24
Yet I still belong to you; you are holding my right hand. You will keep on guiding me with your counsel, leading me to a glorious destiny.

Psalm 119:105
Your word is a lamp for my feet and a light for my path.

Proverbs 6:23
For these commands and this teaching are a lamp to light the way ahead of you. The correction of discipline is the way to life.

James 1:5
If you need wisdom—if you want to know what God wants you to do—ask him, and he will gladly tell you. He will not resent your asking.

The Word of God is from the mind and heart of God—and no one can deny that God is the best guide of all, because he is completely wise, totally powerful, and always with us.

How can the Bible give me comfort?

Psalm 119:49-50, 52, 54
Remember your promise to me, for it is my only hope. Your promise revives me; it comforts me in all my troubles. . . .
I meditate on your age-old laws; O Lord, they comfort me. . . .
Your principles have been the music of my life throughout the years of my pilgrimage.

Proverbs 30:5
Every word of God proves true. He defends all who come to him for protection.

Romans 15:4
Such things were written in the Scriptures long ago to teach us. They give us hope and encouragement as we wait patiently for God's promises.

The Bible is filled with God's promises, which give us comfort and encouragement, as well as the confident assurance that we will one day live forever in peace and safety with him.

PROMISE FROM GOD:

Psalm 119:89
Forever, O Lord, your word stands firm in heaven.

Blame

Is blaming others sin?

Genesis 3:12-13
"Yes," Adam admitted, "but it was the woman you gave me who brought me the fruit, and I ate it." Then the Lord God asked the woman, "How could you do such a thing?" "The serpent tricked me," she replied. "That's why I ate it."

We often want to blame others for our sin. But God knows our heart and is not fooled when we try to take the blame off ourselves.

What can I do to live a blameless life?

1 Corinthians 1:8
He will keep you strong right up to the end, and he will keep you free from all blame on the great day when our Lord Jesus Christ returns.

Colossians 1:22
Now he has brought you back as his friends. He has done this through his death on the cross in his own human body. As a result, he has brought you into the very presence of God, and you are holy and blameless as you stand before him without a single fault.

There is no way that we alone could ever live a blameless life. It is only through Christ's dying on the cross that we are found blameless.

Since it is impossible for me to live perfectly, am I freed of responsibility for my actions?

Philippians 2:15
You are to live clean, innocent lives as children of God in a dark world full of crooked and perverse people. Let your lives shine brightly before them.

••• Our responsibility is to live by Christ's example. We are to keep our heart and mind pure. Imperfection is no excuse for sinning!

PROMISE FROM GOD:

1 Thessalonians 3:13
Christ will make your hearts strong, blameless, and holy when you stand before God our Father on that day when our Lord Jesus comes with all those who belong to him.

••• *Boredom* •••

How do we get bored?

Hebrews 6:11-12
Our great desire is that you will keep right on loving others as long as life lasts, in order to make certain that what you hope for will come true. Then you will not become spiritually dull and indifferent. Instead, you will follow the example of those who are going to inherit God's promises because of their faith and patience.

••• We get bored when we lose hope. It is hope that helps us not give up even when things are difficult.

What are signs of boredom?

Galatians 6:9
Don't get tired of doing what is good. Don't get discouraged and give up, for we will reap a harvest of blessing at the appropriate time.

Proverbs 26:14
As a door turns back and forth on its hinges, so the lazy person turns over in bed.

Ecclesiastes 2:23
Their days of labor are filled with pain and grief; even at night they cannot rest. It is all utterly meaningless.

Getting tired of what is good, feeling like nothing matters, and laziness—these are all signs of boredom.

What gets rid of boredom?

Romans 5:11
Now we can rejoice in our wonderful new relationship with God—all because of what our Lord Jesus Christ has done for us in making us friends of God.

Romans 8:28
We know that God causes everything to work together for the good of those who love God and are called according to his purpose for them.

Ephesians 5:1-2
Follow God's example in everything you do. . . . Live a life filled with love for others, following the example of Christ.

God has a plan for each of us. Boredom disappears when our relationship with God grows to where we recognize his purpose for us. If we really try to follow Christ's example every day, we will never become bored!

PROMISE FROM GOD:

Nehemiah 8:10
The joy of the Lord is your strength!

Challenges

In a world that seems to be against God, how do I handle the challenge of keeping my faith strong?

Psalm 40:12
Troubles surround me—too many to count! They pile up so high I can't see my way out. They are more numerous than the hairs on my head. I have lost all my courage.

1 Chronicles 28:20
Be strong and courageous, and do the work. Don't be afraid or discouraged by the size of the task, for the Lord God, my God, is with you. He will not fail you or forsake you.

Hebrews 6:18
God has given us both his promise and his oath. These two things are unchangeable because it is impossible for God to lie. Therefore, we who have fled to him for refuge can take new courage, for we can hold on to his promise with confidence.

The strength to handle adversity comes from God alone. Therefore we must stay close to him through Bible study and prayer, never doubting his promises.

What can I do when someone challenges me?

Proverbs 15:31-32
If you listen to constructive criticism, you will be at home

among the wise. If you reject criticism, you only harm yourself; but if you listen to correction, you grow in understanding.

Galatians 2:11
When Peter came to Antioch, I had to oppose him publicly, speaking strongly against what he was doing, for it was very wrong.

●●● When someone challenges sin in our life, we must humbly look inside ourselves to determine whether the criticism is true. We should be grateful to those who challenge us to live a godly life, and learn to know when someone's challenge isn't true.

What if someone dares or challenges me to do wrong?

Joshua 1:7
Be strong and very courageous. Obey all the laws Moses gave you. Do not turn away from them, and you will be successful in everything you do.

2 Corinthians 13:8
Our responsibility is never to oppose the truth, but to stand for the truth at all times.

●●● Sin often seems very fun. If it didn't, we wouldn't want to sin. One of our greatest challenges is to do right even when we face temptation, especially when the temptation comes from friends.

How does God challenge us?

Mark 10:21
Jesus felt genuine love for this man as he looked at him. "You lack only one thing," he told him. "Go and sell all you have and

give the money to the poor, and you will have treasure in heaven. Then come, follow me."

God challenges us to search our heart and make sure he has first place in our life.

PROMISE FROM GOD:

Psalm 37:5
Commit everything you do to the Lord. Trust him, and he will help you.

Character

I want to have good character, but some of my friends laugh at me for my "clean living."

1 Corinthians 15:33
Don't be fooled by those who say such things, for "bad company corrupts good character."

If our friends' influence keeps us from having good character, the answer is to get different friends who share godly values.

Can't I work on my character when I get older?

1 Timothy 4:12
Don't let anyone think less of you because you are young. Be an example to all believers in what you teach, in the way you live, in your love, your faith, and your purity.

Godly character is simply a reflection of who we are. If you aren't interested in developing godly character now, you won't be interested in it later.

What qualities are found in godly character?

Ezekiel 18:5-9
Suppose a certain man is just and does what is lawful and right, and he has not feasted in the mountains before Israel's idols or worshiped them. And suppose he . . . does not rob the poor but instead gives food to the hungry and provides clothes for people in need. And suppose he . . . is honest and fair when judging others, and faithfully obeys my laws and regulations. Anyone who does these things is just and will surely live, says the Sovereign Lord.

Godly character involves treating others right.

Galatians 5:22-23
When the Holy Spirit controls our lives, he will produce this kind of fruit in us: love, joy, peace, patience, kindness, goodness, faithfulness, gentleness, and self-control.

Godly character includes all of the fruit of the Spirit.

How can I develop my character?

Deuteronomy 8:2
Remember how the Lord your God led you through the wilderness for forty years, humbling you and testing you to prove your character, and to find out whether or not you would really obey his commands.

James 1:4
So let [your endurance] grow, for when your endurance is fully developed, you will be strong in character and ready for anything.

We are not born with godly character; it is developed. We develop our character by facing daily challenges and choosing wisely.

PROMISE FROM GOD:

Romans 5:4
Endurance develops strength of character in us.

Cheating

What does God think of cheating?

Proverbs 11:1
The Lord hates cheating, but he delights in honesty.

Cheating is the opposite of honesty because the motives behind it are always to deceive someone else. How can anyone trust a cheater?

Can we cheat ourselves?

Luke 16:10
Unless you are faithful in small matters, you won't be faithful in large ones. If you cheat even a little, you won't be honest with greater responsibilities.

When we cheat, we are actually cheating ourselves out of what God has planned for us.

How do we cheat God?

Malachi 3:8
Should people cheat God? Yet you have cheated me! But you ask, "What do you mean? When did we ever cheat you?" You have cheated me of the tithes and offerings due to me.

We cheat God when we don't give him what he rightfully deserves.

PROMISE FROM GOD:

Psalm 9:8
He will judge the world with justice and rule the nations with fairness.

Choices

How do I know if I am making good or bad choices?

Genesis 13:10-13
Lot took a long look at the fertile plains of the Jordan Valley in the direction of Zoar. The whole area was well watered everywhere. . . . Lot chose that land for himself. . . . Lot moved his tents to a place near Sodom, among the cities of the plain. The people of this area were unusually wicked and sinned greatly against the Lord.

2 Peter 2:8
[Lot] was a righteous man who was distressed by the wickedness he saw and heard day after day.

Genesis 19:15, 30
The angels said to Lot, "Get out of here right now, or you will be caught in the destruction of the city." Afterward Lot . . . went to live in a cave in the mountains.

Genesis 25:33-34
Esau swore an oath, thereby selling all his rights as the firstborn to his younger brother. Then Jacob gave Esau some bread and lentil stew. Esau ate and drank and went on about his business, indifferent to the fact that he had given up his birthright.

If our choices are being guided primarily by selfishness

or greed, it is very likely that we, like Lot and Esau, are making bad decisions.

1 Kings 12:8
Rehoboam rejected the advice of the elders and instead asked the opinion of the young men who had grown up with him and who were now his advisers.

Proverbs 12:15
Fools think they need no advice, but the wise listen to others.

●●● If we reject the advice of wise people, like Rehoboam did, we are probably making a very foolish decision. But if we listen carefully to advice, we are more likely to make good choices.

Proverbs 1:7
Fear of the Lord is the beginning of knowledge. Only fools despise wisdom and discipline.

●●● If our decisions are being guided by reverence for God, then we are on our way to making good choices.

Matthew 16:26
How do you benefit if you gain the whole world but lose your own soul in the process? Is anything worth more than your soul?

●●● If our choices are guided by a desire to be accepted by the world and its standards, then we are probably going to make some very bad decisions.

John 5:19
Jesus replied, "I assure you, the Son can do nothing by himself. He does only what he sees the Father doing."

●●● If we, like Jesus, keep in mind what God would have us

do, then we are more likely to make good choices that honor him.

Galatians 5:22-23
When the Holy Spirit controls our lives, he will produce this kind of fruit in us: love, joy, peace, patience, kindness, goodness, faithfulness, gentleness, and self-control. Here there is no conflict with the law.

Good choices always show the fruit of the Holy Spirit, while bad choices often involve rejecting his help in our heart.

PROMISE FROM GOD:

Psalm 23:3
He guides me along right paths, bringing honor to his name.

Church

Why should I go to church?

Psalm 27:4
The one thing I ask of the Lord—the thing I seek most—is to live in the house of the Lord all the days of my life, delighting in the Lord's perfections and meditating in his Temple.

Psalm 84:4
How happy are those who can live in your house, always singing your praises.

Even though God lives in the heart of every believer, he commands us to gather with other believers. When we do that, we meet with God in a special way.

Ephesians 2:19-22
You are members of God's family. We are his house, built on the foundation of the apostles and the prophets. And the cornerstone is Christ Jesus himself. We who believe are carefully joined together, becoming a holy temple for the Lord. Through him you Gentiles are also joined together as part of this dwelling where God lives by his Spirit.

All believers together form God's family, God's house, God's temple, and we are joined together. But only by meeting together can we experience this reality.

Hebrews 10:25
Let us not neglect our meeting together, as some people do, but encourage and warn each other, especially now that the day of his coming back again is drawing near.

When we meet together, we can build each other up and help each other. But we can't experience this kind of fellowship if we don't meet with others!

How is the church supposed to work together?

Romans 12:4-6
Just as our bodies have many parts and each part has a special function, so it is with Christ's body. We are all parts of his one body, and each of us has different work to do. And since we are all one body in Christ, we belong to each other, and each of us needs all the others. God has given each of us the ability to do certain things well.

Ephesians 4:16
Under his direction, the whole body is fitted together perfectly. As each part does its own special work, it helps the

other parts grow, so that the whole body is healthy and growing and full of love.

••• God intends the different members of the body to find their place and to function in their particular area of ministry so that the body can be spiritually healthy.

Ephesians 4:3-6
Always keep yourselves united in the Holy Spirit, and bind yourselves together with peace. We are all one body, we have the same Spirit, and we have all been called to the same glorious future. There is only one Lord, one faith, one baptism, and there is only one God and Father, who is over us all and in us all and living through us all.

••• God wants unity and peace in the church because this shows the truth about Jesus and the Bible.

PROMISE FROM GOD:

Matthew 16:18
Upon this rock I will build my church, and all the powers of hell will not conquer it.

••• Compassion •••

How does God show his compassion to me?

Psalm 103:8
The Lord is merciful and gracious; he is slow to get angry and full of unfailing love.

Psalm 103:13
The Lord is like a father to his children, tender and compassionate to those who fear him.

God shows his compassion to us by giving us blessings we don't deserve and by not giving us the punishment we do deserve for our sins. Instead, he forgives us and helps us grow into what he wants us to be.

How can I show compassion to others?

2 Corinthians 8:9

You know how full of love and kindness our Lord Jesus Christ was. Though he was very rich, yet for your sakes he became poor, so that by his poverty he could make you rich.

Christ in his love for us gave up his most high position to come to earth and die for us. Knowing that should make us want to show compassion to those around us, even when it doesn't feel comfortable.

PROMISE FROM GOD:

Psalm 72:12

He will rescue the poor when they cry to him; he will help the oppressed, who have no one to defend them.

Competition

Is competition good or bad?

1 Corinthians 9:24

Remember that in a race everyone runs, but only one person gets the prize. You also must run in such a way that you will win.

1 Corinthians 15:10

Whatever I am now, it is all because God poured out his special favor on me—and not without results. For I have worked harder than all the other apostles, yet it was not I but God who was working through me by his grace.

••• Competition can drive us to improve ourselves or sharpen our skills. Paul certainly was competitive, and God used this in his life to reach people and build churches throughout the world.

When does competition become a bad thing?

2 Timothy 2:5
Follow the Lord's rules for doing his work, just as an athlete either follows the rules or is disqualified and wins no prize.

Genesis 4:4-5, 8
The Lord accepted Abel and his offering, but he did not accept Cain and his offering. This made Cain very angry and dejected. . . . Later Cain suggested to his brother, Abel, "Let's go out into the fields." And while they were there, Cain attacked and killed his brother.

••• Too much competitiveness can lead to jealousy, anger, and bitterness, causing us to sin.

Luke 18:11
The proud Pharisee stood by himself and prayed this prayer: "I thank you, God, that I am not a sinner like everyone else, especially like that tax collector over there! For I never cheat, I don't sin, I don't commit adultery."

••• Competition can lead us to compare ourselves with others. This is pride, and pride always leads us toward trouble.

Are there areas where competition isn't good?

Matthew 18:1-4
About that time the disciples came to Jesus and asked, "Which of us is greatest in the Kingdom of Heaven?". . . Then [Jesus] said, "Anyone who becomes as humble as this little child is the greatest in the Kingdom of Heaven."

None of us is worth more to God than anyone else; he cares about all of us equally. Competition becomes bad anytime it causes us to think we are more important than others.

People say I can be too competitive at times. How can I learn to lighten up?

Matthew 6:19-20
Don't store up treasures here on earth. . . . Store your treasures in heaven.

We are warned not to spend our life competing for the wrong things or for the wrong reasons.

Colossians 3:23
Work hard and cheerfully at whatever you do, as though you were working for the Lord rather than for people.

We should work hard to do our best, not to beat others. Our best honors God, who created us.

PROMISE FROM GOD:

1 Corinthians 15:57
How we thank God, who gives us victory over sin and death through Jesus Christ our Lord!

Complaining

What's so wrong about complaining?

Numbers 11:1
The people soon began to complain to the Lord about their hardships; and when the Lord heard them, his anger blazed against them. Fire from the Lord raged among them and destroyed the outskirts of the camp.

Numbers 14:27-30
How long will this wicked nation complain about me? I have heard everything the Israelites have been saying. Now tell them this: "As surely as I live, I will do to you the very things I heard you say. I, the Lord, have spoken! You will all die here in this wilderness! Because you complained against me, none of you who are twenty years old or older and were counted in the census will enter the land I swore to give you."

1 Corinthians 10:10
Don't grumble as some of them did, for that is why God sent his angel of death to destroy them.

God considers complaining a sin because it shows an attitude of ungratefulness.

Deuteronomy 6:16
Do not test the Lord your God as you did when you complained at Massah.

Complaining often tests God and his patience.

Job 10:1
I am disgusted with my life. Let me complain freely. I will speak in the bitterness of my soul.

Complaining reveals bitterness.

Psalm 106:25
Instead, they grumbled in their tents and refused to obey the Lord.

••• Complaining can lead to more disobedience.

What should I do instead of complaining?

Philippians 2:14-15
In everything you do, stay away from complaining and arguing, so that no one can speak a word of blame against you. You are to live clean, innocent lives as children of God in a dark world full of crooked and perverse people. Let your lives shine brightly before them.

••• Instead of complaining about others, be a role model to them. Role modeling at its best lifts others up, while complaining puts them down.

Lamentations 3:39-40
Then why should we, mere humans, complain when we are punished for our sins? Instead, let us test and examine our ways. Let us turn again in repentance to the Lord.

••• Instead of complaining about the sins of others, we ought to ask forgiveness for our own sins.

Luke 6:37
Stop judging others, and you will not be judged. Stop criticizing others, or it will all come back on you. If you forgive others, you will be forgiven.

••• Instead of complaining about the faults of others, we ought to forgive them as we would like to be forgiven.

How should I react when others complain about me?

Proverbs 15:31-32
If you listen to constructive criticism, you will be at home among the wise. If you reject criticism, you only harm yourself; but if you listen to correction, you grow in understanding.

Proverbs 25:12
Valid criticism is as treasured by the one who heeds it as jewelry made from finest gold.

Proverbs 29:1
Whoever stubbornly refuses to accept criticism will suddenly be broken beyond repair.

We should always listen to someone's caring criticism and seek to learn and grow from it.

PROMISE FROM GOD:

Proverbs 12:18
The words of the wise bring healing.

Confidence

How can I be more confident?

Genesis 1:26
God said, "Let us make people in our image, to be like ourselves. They will be masters over all life—the fish in the sea, the birds in the sky, and all the livestock, wild animals, and small animals."

Everyone faces times when they are not feeling confident, when they feel insignificant. When these times arise,

remember that God created you in his image and you have many of the characteristics of God himself. He created you with a purpose. Criticizing yourself is criticizing the wonderful way God has made you.

2 Corinthians 5:15
He died for everyone so that those who receive his new life will no longer live to please themselves. Instead, they will live to please Christ, who died and was raised for them.

God loves us so much that he sent his Son, Jesus, to die for us. He didn't die just for the rich or influential, but for everyone, no matter what their station in life. This alone should give us a great sense of self-worth!

PROMISE FROM GOD:

Jeremiah 17:7
Blessed are those who trust in the Lord and have made the Lord their hope and confidence.

Conflict

How should I help when others are in a conflict?

Proverbs 26:17
Yanking a dog's ears is as foolish as interfering in someone else's argument.

It is sometimes tempting to get into an argument between others in order to "solve it," but doing so often only makes things worse.

Romans 12:18
Do your part to live in peace with everyone, as much as possible.

••• As Christ's people we need to work at living in peace with others.

Ephesians 4:3
Always keep yourselves united in the Holy Spirit, and bind yourselves together with peace.

••• Paying attention to the Holy Spirit's leading will often help us to bring peace to our relationships.

What is the right way to handle conflict or disagreement?

Genesis 13:8-9
Then Abram talked it over with Lot. "This arguing between our herdsmen has got to stop," he said. "After all, we are close relatives! I'll tell you what we'll do. Take your choice of any section of the land you want, and we will separate. If you want that area over there, then I'll stay here. If you want to stay in this area, then I'll move on to another place."

1 Corinthians 6:7
To have such lawsuits at all is a real defeat for you. Why not just accept the injustice and leave it at that? Why not let yourselves be cheated?

••• Like Abram, we might have to give up what we want in order to solve a conflict.

John 17:21
My prayer for all of them is that they will be one, just as you and I are one, Father—that just as you are in me and I am in you, so they will be in us, and the world will believe you sent me.

••• We should pray for peace with other people.

Acts 15:37-39
Barnabas . . . wanted to take along John Mark. But Paul disagreed strongly, since John Mark had deserted them in Pamphylia. . . . Their disagreement over this was so sharp that they separated.

••• Sometimes differences of opinion are so strong that no solution seems possible and those people need to stay away from each other.

2 Timothy 2:24-25
The Lord's servants must not quarrel but must be kind to everyone. They must be able to teach effectively and be patient with difficult people. They should gently teach those who oppose the truth.

••• When people disagree with what we are saying, instead of becoming angry and defensive, we should show a kind and gentle attitude.

PROMISE FROM GOD:

Psalm 55:18
He rescues me and keeps me safe from the battle waged against me, even though many still oppose me.

••• Conscience •••

What exactly is our conscience, and where does it come from?

Romans 1:19-20
The truth about God is known to them instinctively. God has

put this knowledge in their hearts. From the time the world was created, people have seen the earth and sky and all that God made. They can clearly see his invisible qualities—his eternal power and divine nature. So they have no excuse whatsoever for not knowing God.

When God created humans, he created them in his image. This makes us unique compared with the rest of God's creation. Conscience is the knowledge God gives us deep inside that guides us between right and wrong. It's the part of us that helps us understand whether we are doing what pleases God.

If God created everyone with a conscience, why have some people done such horrible things?

1 Timothy 1:19

Cling tightly to your faith in Christ, and always keep your conscience clear. For some people have deliberately violated their consciences; as a result, their faith has been shipwrecked.

If we keep going against what our conscience tells us, our conscience can become dull, making us more likely to sin.

Can you lose your conscience?

Proverbs 28:17

A murderer's tormented conscience will drive him into the grave. Don't protect him!

You can't lose your conscience, but if you ignore it long enough you can become dull to its guidance. Then you may not even be able to hear your conscience. Even those

who have done horrible things still have a conscience. But over time they've learned to tune it out. This is so dangerous, because without your conscience you feel free to do whatever you want.

How can I develop my conscience?

Hosea 12:6
So now, come back to your God! Act on the principles of love and justice, and always live in confident dependence on your God.

Even those who have rejected God can come back to him. When you commit yourself to God and live by the commands in his Word, he will strengthen your conscience.

PROMISE FROM GOD:

Psalm 119:105
Your word is a lamp for my feet and a light for my path.

Consequences

Does sin always have negative consequences?

Isaiah 30:12-13
This is the reply of the Holy One of Israel: "Because you despise what I tell you and trust instead in oppression and lies, calamity will come upon you suddenly. It will be like a bulging wall that bursts and falls. In an instant it will collapse and come crashing down.

Lamentations 1:9
She defiled herself with immorality with no thought of the

punishment that would follow. Now she lies in the gutter with no one to lift her out.

●●● It may seem for a time that sin does not have consequences, but sooner or later consequences always come.

Ezekiel 44:12
They encouraged my people to worship other gods, causing Israel to fall into deep sin. So I have raised my hand and taken an oath that they must bear the consequences for their sins, says the Sovereign Lord.

Micah 2:3
This is what the Lord says: "I will reward your evil with evil; you won't be able to escape!"

●●● God has promised that those who sin will face the consequences of what they do.

1 Corinthians 3:13-15
There is going to come a time of testing at the judgment day to see what kind of work each builder has done. Everyone's work will be put through the fire to see whether or not it keeps its value. If the work survives the fire, that builder will receive a reward. But if the work is burned up, the builder will suffer great loss. The builders themselves will be saved, but like someone escaping through a wall of flames.

●●● Some of the consequences of sin will not be felt until the Day of Judgment. Even those who have salvation through Jesus Christ will feel the consequences of their sin.

Galatians 6:8
Those who live only to satisfy their own sinful desires will harvest the consequences of decay and death. But those who live to please the Spirit will harvest everlasting life from the Spirit.

Sin always has negative consequences, but the reverse is also true: Living to please God always has positive consequences.

Do we ever suffer the consequences of another person's sin?

Romans 5:12
Adam's sin brought death, so death spread to everyone, for everyone sinned.

We do suffer the consequences of Adam's sin, but it is also our own sin—we, too, have sinned and deserve the death that he brought.

Isaiah 10:1-2
Destruction is certain for the unjust judges, for those who issue unfair laws. They deprive the poor, the widows, and the orphans of justice. Yes, they rob widows and fatherless children!

The poor, the widows, and the orphans sometimes have to live with the reality of others' sins, but God will make certain that justice is done and that those who sin will deal with the consequences of their own wrongs.

Ezekiel 18:20
The one who sins is the one who dies. The child will not be punished for the parent's sins, and the parent will not be punished for the child's sins. Righteous people will be rewarded for their own goodness, and wicked people will be punished for their own wickedness.

Someday those who sin and those who do good will each receive the consequences of their own actions.

PROMISE FROM GOD:

Romans 6:23
The wages of sin is death, but the free gift of God is eternal life through Christ Jesus our Lord.

◦ ◦ ◦ *Cooperation* ◦ ◦ ◦

Why is it that even though I love God, I find it difficult to obey him all the time?

Jonah 1:1-3
The Lord gave this message to Jonah. . . . "Get up and go to the great city of Nineveh! Announce my judgment against it because I have seen how wicked its people are." But Jonah got up and went in the opposite direction.

◦◦◦ Sometimes fear keeps us from following God—fear of failure, fear of being made fun of for our faith, fear of suffering. When God asks you to do something, don't let fear get in the way.

Romans 7:15
I don't understand myself at all, for I really want to do what is right, but I don't do it. Instead, I do the very thing I hate.

◦◦◦ Even Paul found himself struggling with his old sinful nature. At those times we have the power of the Holy Spirit to help us do what is right.

How should I respond when it's difficult to cooperate with others?

Exodus 17:12-13
Moses' arms finally became too tired to hold up the staff any

longer. So Aaron and Hur found a stone for him to sit on. Then they stood on each side, holding up his hands until sunset. As a result, Joshua and his troops were able to crush the army of Amalek.

••• Moses and Aaron did not always see eye to eye, but in this instance of cooperation, the result was a win for the Israelites. When we do cooperate with each other, God can do amazing things through us.

Proverbs 27:17
As iron sharpens iron, a friend sharpens a friend.

••• Disagreements can produce good results—they can help us see new ideas that might help us grow.

1 Corinthians 1:10
Dear brothers and sisters, I appeal to you by the authority of the Lord Jesus Christ to stop arguing among yourselves. Let there be real harmony so there won't be divisions in the church. I plead with you to be of one mind, united in thought and purpose.

••• Loving confrontation is different from argumentativeness. Conflict will happen; when it happens, true cooperation aims for the best for everyone.

PROMISE FROM GOD:

Psalm 133:1
How wonderful it is, how pleasant, when brothers live together in harmony!

○○○ Courage ○○○

Where do I get the courage to go on when things seem too hard or obstacles seem too big?

Deuteronomy 20:1
The Lord your God . . . is with you!

Psalm 27:1
The Lord is my light and my salvation—so why should I be afraid?

Isaiah 41:10
Don't be afraid, for I am with you. Do not be dismayed, for I am your God. I will strengthen you. I will help you. I will uphold you with my victorious right hand.

Joshua 1:9
Be strong and courageous! Do not be afraid or discouraged. For the Lord your God is with you wherever you go.

○○○ True courage comes from God, from understanding that he is stronger than our mightiest enemies and wants to use his strength to help us.

How do I find the courage to face change?

Genesis 46:3
Do not be afraid to go down to Egypt, for I will see to it that you become a great nation there.

○○○ Change may be part of God's plan for us. If so, we can trust God to take care of us through the changes.

Exodus 4:13
But Moses again pleaded, "Lord, please! Send someone else."

●●● Fear is normal. Being paralyzed by fear, however, can be a sign that you doubt God's ability to care for you during the change.

2 Samuel 4:1
When Ishbosheth heard about Abner's death at Hebron, he lost all courage, and his people were paralyzed with fear.

●●● If you get all of your courage from another person, you'll be left with nothing when that person is gone. If you trust in God, you'll have the strength to go on even when circumstances collapse around you.

How can I find the courage to admit my mistakes?

2 Samuel 12:13
Then David confessed to Nathan, "I have sinned against the Lord." Nathan replied, "Yes, but the Lord has forgiven you."

●●● Admitting our mistakes and sins opens the door to forgiveness and helps repair relationships.

Are there consequences for a lack of courage?

Luke 23:23-24
Their voices prevailed. So Pilate sentenced Jesus to die as they demanded.

●●● Standing up for what's right can get you into trouble with bad people. Not standing up for what's right can get you into trouble with God.

PROMISE FROM GOD:

Joshua 1:9
I command you—be strong and courageous! Do not be afraid or discouraged. For the Lord your God is with you wherever you go.

Criticism

How should I respond to criticism? How do I evaluate whether criticism is constructive or destructive?

Proverbs 12:16-18
A wise person stays calm when insulted. An honest witness tells the truth; a false witness tells lies. Some people make cutting remarks, but the words of the wise bring healing.

If you are criticized, stay calm and don't fight back. Figure out whether the criticism is coming from a person who is known for telling the truth or telling lies. Ask yourself if the criticism is meant to heal or to hurt.

Ecclesiastes 7:5
It is better to be criticized by a wise person than to be praised by a fool!

Measure criticism according to the character of the person who is giving it.

1 Corinthians 4:4
My conscience is clear, but that isn't what matters. It is the Lord himself who will examine me and decide.

Always work to keep a clear conscience by being

honest and trustworthy. This allows you to shrug off criticism that you know isn't true.

1 Peter 4:14
Be happy if you are insulted for being a Christian, for then the glorious Spirit of God will come upon you.

Consider it a privilege to be criticized for your faith in God. God has special blessings for those who patiently endure this kind of criticism.

How can I benefit from constructive criticism?

Proverbs 15:31
If you listen to constructive criticism, you will be at home among the wise.

We keep ourselves from growing when we reject truthful constructive criticism. Sometimes it's painful to hear the truth, but it's worse to ignore it and move into the future without improvement.

Does the Bible give us any warnings about criticizing others?

Romans 14:10
Why do you condemn another Christian? . . . Remember, each of us will stand personally before the judgment seat of God.

James 4:11
If you criticize each other and condemn each other, then you are criticizing and condemning God's law.

Constructive criticism should always be welcomed if it is given in a loving way. But we have no right to give mean

and hurtful criticism to someone else, because that's trying to be a judge over that person, and only God is our judge.

How can we prevent wrong criticism against us?

Romans 14:18
If you serve Christ with this attitude, you will please God. And other people will approve of you, too.

Matthew 7:1
Stop judging others, and you will not be judged.

••• We can usually avoid others' criticisms by acting kindly and showing care for others. But even then, some people will criticize us simply because we are followers of God.

How should we give criticism when it's necessary?

John 8:7
Let those who have never sinned throw the first stones!

Romans 2:1
When you say they are wicked and should be punished, you are condemning yourself, for you do these very same things.

••• Before criticizing someone else, take a look at your own sins and faults so that you can be humble, kind, and understanding when you talk to that person.

1 Corinthians 13:5
Love does not demand its own way. Love is not irritable, and it keeps no record of when it has been wronged.

••• Constructive criticism must always be offered in love, with a desire to build up that other person.

PROMISE FROM GOD:

1 Peter 4:14
Be happy if you are insulted for being a Christian, for then the glorious Spirit of God will come upon you.

Cults

What is a cult?

Judges 2:19
When the judge died, the people returned to their corrupt ways, behaving worse than those who had lived before them. They followed other gods, worshipping and bowing down to them. And they refused to give up their evil practices and stubborn ways.

A cult is a group of people who worship and commit their lives to anything or anyone other than God. Cults tend to be possessive and separate themselves from society, to practice strange rituals, and to follow a religious system formed by a person who seems to be a strong leader. Cults follow religious practices that are against the Bible.

How can I tell if an organization is a cult?

Matthew 7:15-17
Beware of false prophets who come disguised as harmless sheep, but are really wolves that will tear you apart. You can detect them by the way they act, just as you can identify a tree by its fruit. You don't pick grapes from thornbushes, or figs from thistles. A healthy tree produces good fruit, and an unhealthy tree produces bad fruit.

You must compare the teachings of any religious group with the teachings in the Bible. That's why it is so important to know your Bible. If the teachings of a religious group are contrary to what is found in God's Word, and if they tell you that their way is the only way to true peace and happiness, then you may be dealing with a cult.

Romans 10:9
If you confess with your mouth that Jesus is Lord and believe in your heart that God raised him from the dead, you will be saved.

Cults do not teach that faith in Jesus Christ as Savior and forgiveness of sins through him alone is the only way to heaven.

Daniel 6:7
We administrators, prefects, princes, advisers, and other officials have unanimously agreed that Your Majesty should make a law that will be strictly enforced. Give orders that for the next thirty days anyone who prays to anyone, divine or human—except to Your Majesty—will be thrown to the lions.

There are many danger signs that can warn you that a group is a cult. Jesus said that you can tell a man's heart by his actions. Although Daniel wasn't facing a cult, he was facing a group that was trying to keep him from worshipping God. Cults will try to do the same thing.

PROMISE FROM GOD:

Proverbs 12:19
Truth stands the test of time; lies are soon exposed.

◦◦◦ Decisions ◦◦◦

What must I do to make good decisions?

Psalm 25:4
Show me the path where I should walk, O Lord; point out the right road for me to follow.

◦◦◦ Follow God's direction.

Luke 6:12-13
One day soon afterward Jesus went to a mountain to pray, and he prayed to God all night. At daybreak he called together all of his disciples and chose twelve of them to be apostles.

◦◦◦ Talk to God throughout the day. Pray before making an important decision.

Romans 2:18
Yes, you know what he wants; you know right from wrong because you have been taught his law.

◦◦◦ Read God's Word to find his wisdom.

Proverbs 12:15
Fools think they need no advice, but the wise listen to others.

Psalm 37:30
The godly offer good counsel; they know what is right from wrong.

Proverbs 18:15
Intelligent people are always open to new ideas. In fact, they look for them.

◦◦◦ Listen and be open to good advice.

How does God help us make decisions?

Psalm 25:12
Who are those who fear the Lord? He will show them the path they should choose.

Proverbs 4:5
Learn to be wise, and develop good judgment. Don't forget or turn away from my words.

Philippians 2:13
God is working in you, giving you the desire to obey him and the power to do what pleases him.

••• We should pray for God to give us the desire to obey him and seek his guidance. When we obey, he will guide.

How do I know if I've made a good decision?

2 Timothy 3:16
All Scripture is inspired by God and is useful to teach us what is true and to make us realize what is wrong in our lives. It straightens us out and teaches us to do what is right.

Psalm 79:9
Help us, O God of our salvation! Help us for the honor of your name. Oh, save us and forgive our sins for the sake of your name.

Galatians 5:22-23
When the Holy Spirit controls our lives, he will produce this kind of fruit in us: love, joy, peace, patience, kindness, goodness, faithfulness, gentleness, and self-control. Here there is no conflict with the law.

••• You always make the right decision when you follow the commands God has given in the Bible. Also, always check your motives—are you deciding based on what *you*

want or on what is best for others? Are you making a decision that is helping others or hurting them?

How do my decisions show my character?

Proverbs 14:2
Those who follow the right path fear the Lord; those who take the wrong path despise him.

Your decisions determine your actions, and your actions show what is in your heart.

PROMISE FROM GOD:

Proverbs 3:6
Seek his will in all you do, and he will direct your paths.

Depression

What causes depression?

1 Samuel 16:14
Now the Spirit of the Lord had left Saul, and the Lord sent a tormenting spirit that filled him with depression and fear.

If you turn away from the Lord, depression can easily move into the emptiness in your heart.

Job 30:16
Now my heart is broken. Depression haunts my days.

A broken heart can lead to depression.

Ecclesiastes 4:8
This is the case of a man who is all alone, without a child or a brother, yet who works hard to gain as much wealth as he can.

But then he asks himself, "Who am I working for? Why am I giving up so much pleasure now?" It is all so meaningless and depressing.

ooo If you spend your life on things that don't matter, you are bound to get depressed as you realize that what you're doing doesn't have much lasting value.

Proverbs 13:12
Hope deferred makes the heart sick, but when dreams come true, there is life and joy.

ooo A heart without hope is a heart that can easily become depressed.

How should I handle depression?

Psalm 143:7
Come quickly, Lord, and answer me, for my depression deepens. Don't turn away from me, or I will die.

ooo The Lord's strength in our life is the best cure for depression. But with the Lord's help, we may also seek the best medical help and ask God to use it to heal us.

How does God bring healing to those who are depressed?

Psalm 10:17
Lord, you know the hopes of the helpless. Surely you will listen to their cries and comfort them.

Psalm 23:4
Even when I walk through the dark valley of death, I will not be afraid, for you are close beside me. Your rod and your staff protect and comfort me.

Psalm 34:18
The Lord is close to the brokenhearted; he rescues those who are crushed in spirit.

Psalm 147:3
He heals the brokenhearted, binding up their wounds.

Matthew 5:4
God blesses those who mourn, for they will be comforted.

●●● The power of the Lord's presence can bring healing and comfort.

Can any good come out of depression?

Psalm 126:5
Those who plant in tears will harvest with shouts of joy.

Nehemiah 8:10
Don't be dejected and sad, for the joy of the Lord is your strength!

2 Corinthians 12:9
My power works best in your weakness.

●●● When we are weak, we may be more open to the Lord's strength. When God works through our weakness, we know it's his work and not ours.

How can I help people who are depressed?

2 Corinthians 1:4
He comforts us in all our troubles so that we can comfort others. When others are troubled, we will be able to give them the same comfort God has given us.

Romans 12:15
When others are happy, be happy with them. If they are sad, share their sorrow.

Proverbs 25:20
Singing cheerful songs to a person whose heart is heavy is as bad as stealing someone's jacket in cold weather or rubbing salt in a wound.

••• The best way to help depressed people is to comfort them.

PROMISE FROM GOD:

Matthew 11:28
Then Jesus said, "Come to me, all of you who are weary and carry heavy burdens, and I will give you rest."

••• *Distractions* •••

What is the danger in distractions?

Luke 9:62
But Jesus told him, "Anyone who puts a hand to the plow and then looks back is not fit for the Kingdom of God."

Matthew 14:28-31
Then Peter called to him, "Lord, if it's really you, tell me to come to you by walking on water." "All right, come," Jesus said. So Peter went over the side of the boat and walked on the water toward Jesus. But when he looked around at the high waves, he was terrified and began to sink. "Save me, Lord!" he shouted. Instantly Jesus reached out his hand and grabbed him. "You don't have much faith," Jesus said. "Why did you doubt me?"

••• Distractions take our focus off of Jesus. We can be in the middle of doing great things, but if we take our eyes off of Jesus, we will begin to sink!

How can God use distractions?

Exodus 3:1-4
One day Moses was tending the flock of his father-in-law, Jethro. . . . Suddenly, the angel of the Lord appeared to him as a blazing fire in a bush. Moses was amazed because the bush was engulfed in flames, but it didn't burn up. . . . "Why isn't that bush burning up? I must go over to see this." When the Lord saw that he had caught Moses' attention, God called to him from the bush.

Moses was out on an ordinary day doing his ordinary job! God used the bush, a definite distraction, to get Moses' attention.

Acts 9:3-4
As [Saul] was nearing Damascus on this mission, a brilliant light from heaven suddenly beamed down upon him! He fell to the ground and heard a voice saying to him, "Saul! Saul! Why are you persecuting me?"

God can refocus our sights on *his* ways, distracting us from *our* ways. Paul was on his mission to hurt Christians when God got his attention with a distraction that was even harder to ignore than Moses' bush.

How should I deal with distractions?

Mark 10:17
As he was starting out on a trip, a man came running up to Jesus, knelt down, and asked, "Good Teacher, what should I do to get eternal life?"

Matthew 19:13-15
Some children were brought to Jesus so he could lay his hands on them and pray for them. The disciples told them not to

bother him. But Jesus said, "Let the children come to me. Don't stop them! For the Kingdom of Heaven belongs to such as these." And he put his hands on their heads and blessed them before he left.

Distractions happened all the time in Jesus' ministry. The difference in the way he handled distractions is that he just worked the distractions right into the purpose of his life! In other words, Jesus didn't see them as distractions, just as opportunities to show people his love!

Acts 16:29-32
Trembling with fear, the jailer called for lights and ran to the dungeon and fell down before Paul and Silas. He brought them out and asked, "Sirs, what must I do to be saved?" They replied, "Believe on the Lord Jesus and you will be saved, along with your entire household." Then they shared the word of the Lord with him.

Some of us would have looked at a jail sentence as a definite distraction from our mission for God. Not Paul and Silas! Their mission just continued in the jail cell!

How can we remain focused amid distractions?

Hebrews 12:13
Mark out a straight path for your feet. Then those who follow you, though they are weak and lame, will not stumble and fall but will become strong.

Make clear goals for how you will serve God, and then stick to those goals.

Acts 6:3-4
"Look around among yourselves, brothers, and select seven men

who are well respected and are full of the Holy Spirit and wisdom. We will put them in charge of this business. Then we can spend our time in prayer and preaching and teaching the word."

••• Stay focused on what you do well, and learn to let others handle what they can do better.

Psalm 119:157
Many persecute and trouble me, yet I have not swerved from your decrees.

Daniel 6:13
They told the king, "That man Daniel, one of the captives from Judah, is paying no attention to you or your law. He still prays to his God three times a day."

••• Don't be distracted, even by good things, if they take you away from what you know is right.

Psalm 66:9
Our lives are in his hands, and he keeps our feet from stumbling.

••• Keep your attention focused on the Lord.

Proverbs 4:12
If you live a life guided by wisdom, you won't limp or stumble as you run.

••• Constantly seek wisdom.

PROMISE FROM GOD:

Hebrews 12:13
Mark out a straight path for your feet. Then those who follow you, though they are weak and lame, will not stumble and fall but will become strong.

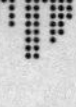

◦◦◦ Doubt ◦◦◦

Sometimes I find myself doubting God and my faith, and I feel ashamed. What can I do?

Psalm 94:19
When doubts filled my mind, your comfort gave me renewed hope and cheer.

Matthew 14:31
Instantly Jesus reached out his hand and grabbed him. "You don't have much faith," Jesus said. "Why did you doubt me?"

◦◦◦ Both David and Peter struggled with doubt. Both men recognized their weakness and humbled themselves before God, and God used them. God doesn't mind doubt as long as we are seeking him for help with our doubt!

Psalm 95:9
There your ancestors tried my patience; they courted my wrath though they had seen my many miracles.

◦◦◦ God gives us plenty of reasons to believe in him. Doubt comes when we ignore those reasons. And when doubt turns to disbelief, we are in danger of ignoring God altogether.

John 20:27
Don't be faithless any longer. Believe!

◦◦◦ Doubt can be healthy or destructive, depending on how we use it. Use your doubts to learn about God and to make your faith stronger.

Are there things we should never doubt?

Ephesians 1:14
The Spirit is God's guarantee that he will give us everything he promised and that he has purchased us to be his own people.

Hebrews 13:5
God has said, "I will never fail you. I will never forsake you."

••• We should never doubt God's promise of salvation. God has promised that as Christians, we will live forever with him in heaven. Satan can never snatch us away from our eternal life with God.

2 Corinthians 6:2
Indeed, God is ready to help you right now.

••• We should never doubt God's desire or ability to help us.

PROMISE FROM GOD:

Hebrews 13:5
God has said, "I will never fail you. I will never forsake you."

••• *Embarrassment* •••

I sometimes lose my temper when I'm embarrassed—is that wrong?

Numbers 22:29
"You have made me look like a fool!" Balaam shouted.

••• Embarrassment often happens when our pride gets hurt. When we are embarrassed, we should figure out if we need to learn something from the experience.

Nehemiah 4:4
Then I prayed, "Hear us, O our God, for we are being mocked."

ooo Nehemiah's response to being mocked was not anger but new prayer and focus on his task.

How should a Christian handle embarrassing situations?

Matthew 1:19
Joseph, her fiancé, being a just man, decided to break the engagement quietly, so as not to disgrace her publicly.

ooo Even when his engagement and personal reputation were on the line, Joseph was careful not to humiliate Mary publicly.

Matthew 14:9
The king was sorry, but because of his oath and because he didn't want to back down in front of his guests, he issued the necessary orders.

ooo We must not allow embarrassment to pressure us into doing what we know is sin.

Sometimes my friends make fun of my Christian faith.

Mark 8:38
If a person is ashamed of me and my message in these adulterous and sinful days, I, the Son of Man, will be ashamed of that person when I return.

ooo We never have to be ashamed or embarrassed about Jesus.

Romans 1:16
I am not ashamed of this Good News about Christ.

Paul was not ashamed of the Good News, which alone holds the power to save souls for all eternity.

2 Timothy 1:8
You must never be ashamed to tell others about our Lord.

Believers should never be embarrassed to tell others about their faith in Christ.

PROMISE FROM GOD:

Psalm 119:80
May I be blameless in keeping your principles; then I will never have to be ashamed.

Encouragement

How does God encourage us?

Genesis 1:27
God created people in his own image; God patterned them after himself; male and female he created them.

1 Peter 2:5
God is building you, as living stones, into his spiritual temple. What's more, you are God's holy priests, who offer the spiritual sacrifices that please him because of Jesus Christ.

1 Corinthians 15:3
I passed on to you what was most important and what had also been passed on to me—that Christ died for our sins, just as the Scriptures said.

God created us, so he knows us and understands that we need encouragement. He values us so much that he was willing to send his Son, Jesus, to die for us because he wants us to live with him forever.

How should we encourage others?

1 Thessalonians 5:11
Encourage each other and build each other up, just as you are already doing.

Romans 14:19
Let us aim for harmony in the church and try to build each other up.

Hebrews 7:7
Without question, the person who has the power to bless is always greater than the person who is blessed.

Galatians 5:13-14
You have been called to live in freedom—not freedom to satisfy your sinful nature, but freedom to serve one another in love. For the whole law can be summed up in this one command: "Love your neighbor as yourself."

We help one another through kind words, acts of service, and building each other up. This gives us a great sense of worth.

PROMISE FROM GOD:

Psalm 67:1
May God be merciful and bless us. May his face shine with favor upon us.

ooo Evil ooo

Why do people often seem to get away with evil?

Jeremiah 12:1-2
Why are the wicked so prosperous? Why are evil people so happy? You have planted them, and they have taken root and prospered. Your name is on their lips, but in their hearts they give you no credit at all.

ooo Even Jeremiah struggled with the success of evil people. We must remember that because of sin, life on this earth isn't fair. But at the final judgment, God will make everything fair for all eternity.

Isaiah 32:7-8
The smooth tricks of evil people will be exposed, including all the lies they use to oppress the poor in the courts. But good people will be generous to others and will be blessed for all they do.

ooo It seems that people today can do anything they want and not only get away with it, but also be better off. But God has promised that in his time everyone will be judged, evil will be exposed, and his people will last forever. God doesn't promise that this world will be free of evil. In fact, he warns that evil will be powerful. But God promises to help us stand against evil, and if we do, we'll receive our reward of eternal life with him in heaven, where evil won't exist anymore.

Why does it sometimes seem tempting to do evil?

Romans 7:16-17
I know perfectly well that what I am doing is wrong, and my bad conscience shows that I agree that the law is good. But I can't help myself, because it is sin inside me that makes me do these evil things.

Paul knew that sin causes us to do evil things even when we're focused on doing right. Sin may seem fun. If it didn't, no one would want to sin. That's why it's so hard to resist.

How can we fight evil?

Romans 12:21
Don't let evil get the best of you, but conquer evil by doing good.

Romans 13:14
Let the Lord Jesus Christ take control of you, and don't think of ways to indulge your evil desires.

We cannot battle evil on our own. Victory over evil can happen only when we listen to the Holy Spirit each day. We fight evil with good. It's one of the hardest things to do, but it's the most powerful.

PROMISE FROM GOD:

Galatians 5:22-23
When the Holy Spirit controls our lives, he will produce this kind of fruit in us: love, joy, peace, patience, kindness, goodness, faithfulness, gentleness, and self-control.

Evolution

If things did not evolve, how were the earth and life formed?

Genesis 1:1
In the beginning God created the heavens and the earth.

Genesis 1:25-26
God made all sorts of wild animals, livestock, and small animals, each able to reproduce more of its own kind. And God saw that it was good. Then God said, "Let us make people in our image, to be like ourselves. They will be masters over all life—the fish in the sea, the birds in the sky, and all the livestock, wild animals, and small animals."

The Bible clearly states that God made the heavens, the earth, and all that lives in it. The Bible doesn't say much about how God did it, but the fact is that he did it.

PROMISE FROM GOD:

Psalm 90:2
Before the mountains were created, before you made the earth and the world, you are God, without beginning or end.

Excuses

Where is the first excuse in the Bible?

Genesis 3:12
It was the woman you gave me who brought me the fruit, and I ate it.

Adam made the first excuse. He blamed Eve, and indirectly he blamed God for giving her to him. Then Eve blamed the serpent. Both tried to excuse their action by blaming someone else.

What are some examples of other people who had poor excuses?

Genesis 16:5
Then Sarai said to Abram, "It's all your fault!"

Sarai (Sarah) couldn't have children, so she gave her slave to Abram in order to have a child through her. Later Sarah had second thoughts and blamed Abram (Abraham) for the whole thing.

Exodus 32:24
When they brought [their gold earrings] to me, I threw them into the fire—and out came this calf!

Aaron's lame excuse for making an idol—something condemned by God—was that it just happened by itself! We often do the same thing, blaming our sin on things we can't control. But we're completely responsible for *all* our actions (Romans 14:12; Revelation 20:12).

1 Samuel 15:15
"It's true that the army spared the best of the sheep and cattle," Saul admitted. "But they are going to sacrifice them to the Lord your God. We have destroyed everything else."

Saul tried to justify his sinful actions with one excuse after another. Finally he ran out of excuses and lost his kingdom (1 Samuel 15:26).

Luke 22:60
Peter said, "Man, I don't know what you are talking about."

••• Peter wanted to save his life or, at least, avoid being mocked for being with Jesus.

Can we ever excuse ourselves from God's work because we don't have the ability?

Exodus 4:10
Moses pleaded with the Lord, "O Lord, I'm just not a good speaker."

Judges 6:15-16
"Lord," Gideon replied, "how can I rescue Israel? My clan is the weakest in the whole tribe of Manasseh, and I am the least in my entire family!" The Lord said to him, "I will be with you."

••• Both Moses and Gideon thought they had a good excuse for not serving God. But the skills God looks for are different from what we might expect. He often chooses the least likely people to do his work in order to demonstrate his power. If you know God wants you to do something, stop trying to excuse yourself. He will give you the help and strength you need to get the job done.

Can anyone be excused for not accepting the Lord?

Philippians 2:10-11
At the name of Jesus every knee will bow . . . and every tongue will confess that Jesus Christ is Lord.

••• We all have excuses for not putting God first—we're too busy, we're not sure how to talk to others about God, we'll do it later, we don't know where to start. Do you think those excuses will hold up when we see God face-to-face?

Romans 1:20
From the time the world was created, people have seen the earth and sky and all that God made. They can clearly see his invisible qualities—his eternal power and divine nature. So they have no excuse whatsoever for not knowing God.

Everyone has at least had the testimony of nature, God's work. That alone shows his presence and power. So people who fail to accept the Lord don't have any excuse.

PROMISE FROM GOD:

1 Peter 1:17
Remember that the heavenly Father to whom you pray has no favorites when he judges. He will judge or reward you according to what you do. So you must live in reverent fear of him during your time as foreigners here on earth.

Failure

See also Success

How do I prevent failure in my life?

Numbers 14:22
Not one of these people will ever enter that land. They have seen my glorious presence and the miraculous signs I performed both in Egypt and in the wilderness, but again and again they tested me by refusing to listen.

Hebrews 4:6
God's rest is there for people to enter. But those who formerly heard the Good News failed to enter because they disobeyed God.

●●● We can prevent failure by listening to God and doing what he says.

Matthew 7:24-27
Anyone who listens to my teaching and obeys me is wise, like a person who builds a house on solid rock. Though the rain comes in torrents and the floodwaters rise and the winds beat against that house, it won't collapse, because it is built on rock. But anyone who hears my teaching and ignores it is foolish, like a person who builds a house on sand. When the rains and floods come and the winds beat against that house, it will fall with a mighty crash.

●●● By listening to Christ and his instructions, we can keep from failing.

1 Chronicles 28:20
Be strong and courageous, and do the work. Don't be afraid or discouraged by the size of the task, for the Lord God, my God, is with you.

●●● When we put our trust completely in God and take courage in his help, we won't fail.

Isaiah 42:23
Will not even one of you apply these lessons from the past and see the ruin that awaits you?

●●● We can avoid failure if we learn from our past mistakes.

When I have failed, how do I get past it and go on?

1 Kings 8:33-34
If your people Israel are defeated by their enemies because they have sinned against you, and if they turn to you and call on

your name and pray to you here in this Temple, then hear from heaven and forgive their sins and return them to this land you gave their ancestors.

••• Apologizing and turning to God for forgiveness is the best response we can have to our own failure.

Micah 7:8
Though I fall, I will rise again. Though I sit in darkness, the Lord himself will be my light.

••• The best response to failure is to get up again, with the hope that comes from believing in God.

PROMISE FROM GOD:

Psalm 37:23-24
The steps of the godly are directed by the Lord. He delights in every detail of their lives. Though they stumble, they will not fall, for the Lord holds them by the hand.

••• Fear •••

What can I do when I am overcome with fear? How do I find the strength to go on?

Psalm 46:1-2
God is our refuge and strength, always ready to help in times of trouble. So we will not fear, even if earthquakes come and the mountains crumble into the sea.

John 14:27
I am leaving you with a gift—peace of mind and heart. . . . So don't be troubled or afraid.

••• God promises to comfort us in our fear if we seek him

when we're afraid. We have the confident assurance that he is always with us no matter what happens.

What does it mean to fear God?

Psalm 2:11
Serve the Lord with reverent fear, and rejoice with trembling.

ooo Because God is so great and mighty, and because he holds the power of life and death in his hands, we must have a healthy, respectful fear of him. A healthy fear helps us stay on track in our relationship with God.

2 Corinthians 7:1
Let us work toward complete purity because we fear God.

ooo A healthy fear of God helps us want to be holy.

Deuteronomy 31:7-8
Be strong and courageous! . . . Do not be afraid or discouraged, for the Lord is the one who goes before you.

ooo Fear can be good if it teaches us about courage. Joshua couldn't have truly understood courage if he hadn't experienced fear. He had courageous character because he depended on and trusted in God even when he was afraid.

When is fear not good?

Genesis 26:7
He was afraid to admit that she was his wife.

Joshua 17:16
The Canaanites . . . have iron chariots—they are too strong for us.

ooo Fear isn't good if it keeps us from doing the things we should do. God does not want us to live in fear.

PROMISE FROM GOD:

Isaiah 41:10
Don't be afraid, for I am with you. Do not be dismayed, for I am your God. I will strengthen you. I will help you. I will uphold you with my victorious right hand.

ooo *Forgiveness* ooo

Do I have to forgive others who hurt me?

Matthew 6:14-15
If you forgive those who sin against you, your heavenly Father will forgive you. But if you refuse to forgive others, your Father will not forgive your sins.

Mark 11:25
When you are praying, first forgive anyone you are holding a grudge against, so that your Father in heaven will forgive your sins, too.

ooo We will receive God's forgiveness only when we forgive others who have wronged us.

Matthew 18:21-22
Peter came to him and asked, "Lord, how often should I forgive someone who sins against me? Seven times?" "No!" Jesus replied, "seventy times seven!"

ooo Just as God forgives us without limit, we should forgive others without counting how many times.

Luke 23:34
Jesus said, "Father, forgive these people, because they don't know what they are doing."

••• Jesus forgave those who mocked him and killed him.

Colossians 3:13
You must make allowance for each other's faults and forgive the person who offends you. Remember, the Lord forgave you, so you must forgive others.

1 Peter 3:9
Don't repay evil for evil. Don't retaliate when people say unkind things about you. Instead, pay them back with a blessing. That is what God wants you to do, and he will bless you for it.

••• God wants us to respond to others' sins by being kind to them.

Is there a limit to how much God will forgive me?

Isaiah 1:18
"Come now, let us argue this out," says the Lord. "No matter how deep the stain of your sins, I can remove it. I can make you as clean as freshly fallen snow. Even if you are stained as red as crimson, I can make you as white as wool."

Joel 2:32
Anyone who calls on the name of the Lord will be saved.

••• No matter how sinful and disobedient we have been, we can receive God's forgiveness by turning to him in repentance.

Psalm 86:5
O Lord, you are so good, so ready to forgive, so full of unfailing love for all who ask your aid.

Psalm 103:3
He forgives all my sins and heals all my diseases.

Ezekiel 18:22
All their past sins will be forgotten, and they will live because of the righteous things they have done.

ooo God is ready to forgive us.

Matthew 18:23-5, 27
The Kingdom of Heaven can be compared to a king who decided to bring his accounts up to date. . . . One of his debtors was brought in who owed him millions of dollars. He couldn't pay. . . . Then the king was filled with pity for him, and he released him and forgave his debt.

ooo God is merciful toward us even though our debt of sin is so great.

Luke 24:47
With my authority, take this message of repentance to all the nations, beginning in Jerusalem: "There is forgiveness of sins for all who turn to me."

Ephesians 1:7
He is so rich in kindness that he purchased our freedom through the blood of his Son, and our sins are forgiven.

Colossians 1:14
God has purchased our freedom with his blood and has forgiven all our sins.

ooo God is willing to forgive every sin because Christ has already paid the penalty for all sin by his death.

Mark 3:29
Anyone who blasphemes against the Holy Spirit will never be forgiven. It is an eternal sin.

●●● Those who harden themselves against God's Spirit and reject him completely will never experience his forgiveness.

PROMISE FROM GOD:

1 John 1:9
If we confess our sins to him, he is faithful and just to forgive us and to cleanse us from every wrong.

●●● *Friendship* ●●●

What is the sign of true friendship?

Proverbs 17:17
A friend is always loyal, and a brother is born to help in time of need.

1 Samuel 18:3
Jonathan made a special vow to be David's friend.

●●● Some friendships last, and others don't. True friendships are glued together with bonds of loyalty and commitment. They remain strong throughout changing circumstances.

What gets in the way of friendships?

1 Samuel 18:9-11
From that time on Saul kept a jealous eye on David. . . . Saul, who had a spear in his hand, suddenly hurled it at David.

●●● Jealousy is the great dividing force of friendships. Envy over what a friend has can quickly turn to anger and bitterness, causing you to separate yourself from the one you truly cared for.

Psalm 41:9
Even my best friend, the one I trusted completely . . . has turned against me.

⚬⚬⚬ When respect or reverence is seriously damaged, even the closest friendship is at risk.

Genesis 50:17-21
"We . . . beg you to forgive us." But Joseph told them . . . "No, don't be afraid. Indeed, I myself will take care of you."

⚬⚬⚬ Forgiveness restores broken relationships.

What should I do when I'm having trouble making friends?

Job 19:19
My close friends abhor me. Those I loved have turned against me.

John 5:7
I have no one to help me into the pool.

⚬⚬⚬ We all go through times when it seems that our friends have left us.

John 15:15
I no longer call you servants. . . . Now you are my friends.

Hebrews 13:5
I will never fail you. I will never forsake you.

⚬⚬⚬ The first thing we must do is remember that God is our constant friend and will never leave us.

Ephesians 4:32
Instead, be kind to each other, tenderhearted, forgiving one another, just as God through Christ has forgiven you.

●●● Acts of kindness and generosity help others learn to like you.

PROMISE FROM GOD:

Matthew 18:20
Where two or three gather together because they are mine, I am there among them.

●●● *Fun* ●●●

Can I be a Christian and still have fun?

Nehemiah 8:10
Go and celebrate with a feast . . . and share gifts of food with people who have nothing prepared. This is a sacred day. . . . Don't be . . . sad, for the joy of the Lord is your strength!

Matthew 25:21
You have been faithful in handling this small amount. . . . Let's celebrate together!

Proverbs 13:9
The life of the godly is full of light and joy, but the sinner's light is snuffed out.

1 Timothy 3:2
He must enjoy having guests in his home.

●●● Joy, fun, and celebration, as God intended, are important parts of Christian faith because these things lift our spirits and help us to see the beauty and meaning in life.

What kinds of things are wrong when having fun?

1 Peter 4:3
You have had enough in the past of the evil things that godless people enjoy . . . their feasting and drunkenness and wild parties.

Fun is wrong when it is self-centered or greedy, when it involves sinful acts, or when it tempts you into sin.

PROMISE FROM GOD:

Psalm 19:8
The commandments of the Lord are right, bringing joy to the heart.

God's Will

Does God have a plan for my life?

Psalm 139:3
You chart the path ahead of me and tell me where to stop and rest. Every moment you know where I am.

God cares about what we do. He cares about the details of our life.

Psalm 138:8
The Lord will work out his plans for my life.

God's plans for us are always for good. Unknown plans can be frightening, but when the plans belong to God, we can rest assured that we can expect something awesome.

Psalm 32:8
The Lord says, "I will guide you along the best pathway for your life. I will advise you and watch over you."

God wants to help us follow the path that will be most pleasing to *him,* not the path that may be the one we think we want.

What can I do to discover God's will for my life?

Proverbs 2:3-5
Cry out for insight and understanding. Search for them as you would for lost money or hidden treasure. Then you will understand what it means to fear the Lord.

Actively look for God's will for you.

Isaiah 2:3
Come, let us go up to the mountain of the Lord, to the Temple of the God of Israel. There he will teach us his ways, so that we may obey him.

Let God teach you from his Word.

Hosea 6:3
Oh, that we might know the Lord! Let us press on to know him! Then he will respond to us.

Give yourself completely to knowing his will. Seek God's will with all your heart, not just part of it.

Proverbs 2:6
The Lord grants wisdom!

James 1:5
If you want to know what God wants you to do—ask him, and he will gladly tell you. He will not resent your asking.

1 John 5:14
We can be confident that he will listen to us whenever we ask him for anything in line with his will.

⚬⚬⚬ Pray, asking God to show his will to you.

Acts 21:14
When it was clear that we couldn't persuade him, we gave up and said, "The will of the Lord be done."

⚬⚬⚬ Sometimes God's will for us becomes clear through circumstances that are beyond our control and in his hands.

What are some of the things that we know are God's will for us?

Amos 5:24
I want to see a mighty flood of justice, a river of righteous living that will never run dry.

⚬⚬⚬ God's will is that we seek justice at all times and that we do what is right.

1 Corinthians 14:1
Let love be your highest goal.

⚬⚬⚬ God's will is that we love others.

Mark 10:45
Even I, the Son of Man, came here not to be served but to serve others.

⚬⚬⚬ God's will is that we serve others, putting them above ourselves.

Exodus 20:1
God instructed the people.

⚬⚬⚬ God's will is that we obey him.

Galatians 5:22
When the Holy Spirit controls our lives, he will produce . . . fruit in us.

○○○ God's will is that we live in the Holy Spirit's power and guidance.

Proverbs 16:3
Commit your work to the Lord, and then your plans will succeed.

○○○ God's will is that we do everything as if we were doing it for him.

PROMISE FROM GOD:

Jeremiah 29:11
"I know the plans I have for you," says the Lord. "They are plans for good and not for disaster, to give you a future and a hope."

○○○ Gossip ○○○

Why is gossip so bad?

Leviticus 19:16
Do not spread slanderous gossip among your people.

○○○ God hates gossip. He commands us not to do it.

Proverbs 11:13
A gossip goes around revealing secrets, but those who are trustworthy can keep a confidence.

○○○ Gossiping often involves breaking another's trust.

Romans 1:29
Their lives became full of every kind of wickedness, sin, greed,

hate, envy, murder, fighting, deception, malicious behavior, and gossip.

○○○ Gossip is so bad that God puts it in the same category as greed, hate, envy, and murder.

1 Timothy 5:13
They are likely to become lazy and spend their time gossiping . . . getting into other people's business and saying things they shouldn't.

○○○ Gossiping often grows out of laziness. When we have nothing better to do than sit around talking about other people, we may wind up saying things we'll later regret.

Matthew 7:1
Stop judging others, and you will not be judged.

○○○ Gossiping puts us in the place of judging others. When we sit as judge, we allow rumors and opinions to damage the reputation of others who aren't there to defend themselves.

Proverbs 18:8
What dainty morsels rumors are—but they sink deep into one's heart.

○○○ Gossip hurts others. If you say things about others that don't turn out to be true, people won't believe what you say later on.

How can I stop gossip?

Proverbs 26:20
Fire goes out for lack of fuel, and quarrels disappear when gossip stops.

••• Stop the chain of gossip with you! When you hear gossip, you can do something about it. You can decide not to spread it any further. Stop the fires of gossip from spreading beyond you.

Deuteronomy 13:14
You must examine the facts carefully.

••• Don't assume that everything you hear is true. Get the facts straight from the right source.

Matthew 7:12
Do for others what you would like them to do for you.

••• The Golden Rule can also be applied to our speech: Talk about others in the same way you would like them to talk about you.

Ephesians 4:29
Let everything you say be good and helpful, so that your words will be an encouragement to those who hear them.

••• If we focus on what is good and helpful, we won't give gossip a place in our heart.

Colossians 3:17
Whatever you do or say, let it be as a representative of the Lord Jesus.

••• If you think you may be about to gossip, ask yourself: *Does the person I'm talking to need to know this? Is it true and helpful?*

PROMISE FROM GOD:

1 Peter 3:10
The Scriptures say, "If you want a happy life and good days, keep your tongue from speaking evil, and keep your lips from telling lies."

Habits

What are some of the bad habits the Bible talks about?

1 John 3:8
When people keep on sinning, it shows they belong to the Devil.

Sin is a habit none of us can beat completely, but a pattern of sinful living shows that we may not be serious about following God.

Exodus 8:28, 32
"All right, go ahead," Pharaoh replied. "I will let you go. . . ." But Pharaoh hardened his heart again and refused to let the people go.

Pharaoh developed a bad habit of lying and wanting his own way. We can easily slip into these same habits, but that is disastrous.

Numbers 11:1
The people soon began to complain . . . about their hardships.

The Israelites developed a bad habit of complaining. That habit can quickly turn into bitterness.

1 Timothy 5:13
They are likely to become lazy and spend their time gossiping.

••• Too much time and too little to do can make it easy to develop the bad habit of gossip.

How should we deal with bad habits?

Romans 7:15
I don't understand myself at all, for I really want to do what is right, but I don't do it. Instead, I do the very thing I hate.

••• Have you ever felt this way? Paul knew that he could not kick the habit of sin overnight. But he knew that, with God's help, he could improve every day. In the same way, we may have to give up a habit in phases, one day at a time.

1 John 2:15
Stop loving this evil world and all that it offers you.

••• Sin often appears to be fun and good. In the same way, bad habits often feel good even though we know they're bad for us. Breaking a bad habit can be hard because we are losing something we like. But pain over losing a bad habit brings a true joy because we're doing what is pleasing to God.

Colossians 3:2
Let heaven fill your thoughts.

••• We must replace a bad habit with something good.

What are some good habits we can develop?

Hebrews 10:25
Let us not neglect our meeting together, as some people do.

ooo Meeting together as believers is a good habit because it provides time with other believers, it develops the habit of group Bible study, it keeps us busy when we might be slipping into bad habits, and it offers help from others in the group.

Genesis 26:21-22
Isaac's men then dug another well, but again there was a fight over it. . . . Abandoning that one, he dug another well, and the local people finally left him alone.

ooo Isaac pursued a habit of peace.

Psalm 28:7
The Lord is my strength, my shield from every danger. I trust in him with all my heart. . . . I burst out in songs of thanksgiving.

ooo As a young boy, David developed the habit of talking to God, singing songs about him, and writing psalms. This helped him to trust and follow God all his life.

PROMISE FROM GOD:

Romans 8:5
Those who are dominated by the sinful nature think about sinful things, but those who are controlled by the Holy Spirit think about things that please the Spirit.

ooo *Happiness* ooo

How can I make God happy?

Deuteronomy 30:10
The Lord your God will delight in you if you obey his voice and keep the commands and laws written in this Book of the

Law, and if you turn to the Lord your God with all your heart and soul.

Proverbs 11:1
The Lord . . . delights in honesty.

Proverbs 11:20
The Lord . . . delights in those who have integrity.

Proverbs 15:8
The Lord . . . delights in the prayers of the upright.

Proverbs 15:26
The Lord . . . delights in pure words.

Can we human beings truly bring joy and delight to the Lord, the Creator of the universe? Yes! We bring delight to God by honoring him, obeying him, responding to his love by loving him, seeking his forgiveness, and spending time with him each day by praying and reading his Word.

How does God show his happiness with me?

Zephaniah 3:17
The Lord your God has arrived to live among you. He is a mighty savior. He will rejoice over you with great gladness. With his love, he will calm all your fears. He will exult over you by singing a happy song.

Psalm 18:19
He led me to a place of safety; he rescued me because he delights in me.

Psalm 149:4
The Lord delights in his people; he crowns the humble with salvation.

ooo The Lord delights in saving us from our sins, guiding us in his ways, and daily taking care of us.

How can we find true happiness?

Psalm 40:16
May all who search for you be filled with joy and gladness. May those who love your salvation repeatedly shout, "The Lord is great!"

Psalm 68:3
Let the godly rejoice. Let them be glad in God's presence. Let them be filled with joy.

Psalm 86:4
Give me happiness, O Lord, for my life depends on you.

Psalm 146:5
Happy are those who have the God of Israel as their helper, whose hope is in the Lord their God.

ooo The Lord himself is the source of true happiness. The more we love him, know him, walk with him, and become like him, the greater our happiness.

How can I bring happiness to others?

Romans 12:10
Love each other with genuine affection, and take delight in honoring each other.

2 Corinthians 7:13
In addition to our own encouragement, we were especially delighted to see how happy Titus was at the way you welcomed him and set his mind at ease.

Ecclesiastes 9:9
Live happily with the woman you love through all the meaningless days of life that God has given you in this world. The wife God gives you is your reward for all your earthly toil.

As we find true happiness through knowing God, we can pass on that happiness to others.

PROMISE FROM GOD:

Proverbs 11:23
The godly can look forward to happiness, while the wicked can expect only wrath.

Heaven

Is there really a heaven?

Genesis 14:22
Abram replied, "I have solemnly promised the Lord, God Most High, Creator of heaven and earth."

John 14:2
There are many rooms in my Father's home, and I am going to prepare a place for you. If this were not so, I would tell you plainly.

2 Corinthians 5:1
For we know that when this earthly tent we live in is taken down—when we die and leave these bodies—we will have a home in heaven.

Not only is there a heaven, but Jesus is getting it ready for Christians.

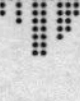

What is heaven like?

Isaiah 65:17
Look! I am creating new heavens and a new earth—so wonderful that no one will even think about the old ones anymore.

Philippians 3:21
He will take these weak mortal bodies of ours and change them into glorious bodies like his own.

James 1:17
Whatever is good and perfect comes to us from God above, who created all heaven's lights.

Revelation 21:3-4
I heard a loud shout from the throne, saying, "Look, the home of God is now among his people! He will live with them, and they will be his people. God himself will be with them. He will remove all of their sorrows, and there will be no more death or sorrow or crying or pain. For the old world and its evils are gone forever."

Revelation 22:5
There will be no night there—no need for lamps or sun—for the Lord God will shine on them. And they will reign forever and ever.

In heaven we will live forever with God. There will be no sadness, no pain, no evil, no death. Everything will be perfect and wonderful. God will give us each a new body, and we'll be able to talk face-to-face with Jesus.

Who will get into heaven?

Matthew 5:3
God blesses those who realize their need for him, for the Kingdom of Heaven is given to them.

Matthew 19:14
Jesus said, "Let the children come to me. Don't stop them! For the Kingdom of Heaven belongs to such as these."

John 3:16
God so loved the world that he gave his only Son, so that everyone who believes in him will not perish but have eternal life.

Those who accept Jesus Christ as Savior and understand that only he can forgive their sins will go to heaven someday.

Does the Bible really say there's only one way to heaven?

John 14:6
Jesus told him, "I am the way, the truth, and the life. No one can come to the Father except through me."

Jesus is the only way to heaven. We may want to buy our way in, work our way in, think our way in. But the Bible is clear—believing in Jesus Christ is the only way in.

PROMISE FROM GOD:

1 Corinthians 2:9
No eye has seen, no ear has heard, and no mind has imagined what God has prepared for those who love him.

Hell

Is there really a place called hell?

Matthew 7:13
You can enter God's Kingdom only through the narrow gate.

The highway to hell is broad, and its gate is wide for the many who choose the easy way.

Matthew 13:49-50
That is the way it will be at the end of the world. The angels will come and separate the wicked people from the godly, throwing the wicked into the fire.

Revelation 20:10
The Devil . . . was thrown into the lake of fire that burns with sulfur. . . . There they will be tormented day and night forever and ever.

Although we don't know where hell is, it definitely exists.

What is hell like?

2 Peter 2:4
God did not spare even the angels when they sinned; he threw them into hell, in gloomy caves and darkness.

Revelation 19:20
Both the beast and his false prophet were thrown alive into the lake of fire that burns with sulfur.

Jude 1:7
Those cities [Sodom and Gomorrah] were destroyed by fire and are a warning of the eternal fire that will punish all who are evil.

Luke 16:22-24
The rich man also died and was buried, and his soul went to the place of the dead. There, in torment, he saw Lazarus in the far distance with Abraham. The rich man shouted, "Father Abraham, have some pity! Send Lazarus over here to dip the tip of his finger in water and cool my tongue, because I am in anguish in these flames."

●●● Our imagination can't understand how horrible hell is. Here on earth we think that everything has a beginning and an end. There will be no end to hell.

Who will be sent to hell?

Jude 1:15
He will bring the people of the world to judgment. He will convict the ungodly of all the evil things they have done in rebellion and of all the insults that godless sinners have spoken against him.

Revelation 20:15
Anyone whose name was not found recorded in the Book of Life was thrown into the lake of fire.

●●● All who don't believe in Jesus for salvation and forgiveness for their sins will spend forever in hell.

How can I be sure that I won't go to hell?

John 14:6
Jesus told him, "I am the way, the truth, and the life. No one can come to the Father except through me."

1 John 4:17
As we live in God, our love grows more perfect. So we will not be afraid on the day of judgment, but we can face him with confidence because we are like Christ here in this world.

Romans 10:9
If you confess with your mouth that Jesus is Lord and believe in your heart that God raised him from the dead, you will be saved.

●●● There's only one way to know for sure that you're going to heaven someday. You must believe that you're

a sinner, ask for God's forgiveness, and believe in Jesus Christ as your personal Savior. By taking this step, you can know you have a place in heaven, and you don't have to be afraid of hell.

PROMISE FROM GOD:

John 3:16
God so loved the world that he gave his only Son, so that everyone who believes in him will not perish but have eternal life.

Honesty

Why is it so important to be honest?

Psalm 24:3-4
Who may climb the mountain of the Lord? Who may stand in his holy place? Only those whose hands and hearts are pure, who do not worship idols and never tell lies.

Honesty is necessary for us to live in God's presence.

Proverbs 16:11
The Lord demands fairness in every business deal; he sets the standard.

God expects us to be honest.

Proverbs 12:5
The plans of the godly are just.

Matthew 12:33
A tree is identified by its fruit.

Luke 16:10
If you cheat even a little, you won't be honest with greater responsibilities.

••• People's honesty or dishonesty shows just what kind of people they are.

1 Timothy 1:19
Always keep your conscience clear. For some people have deliberately violated their consciences; as a result, their faith has been shipwrecked.

••• Honesty keeps a clear conscience, without any guilt.

Proverbs 11:3
Good people are guided by their honesty; treacherous people are destroyed by their dishonesty.

••• Dishonesty is like a trap because we're always trying to hide the truth. Honesty brings a feeling of freedom because it leaves room for forgiveness, good changes, and healing.

Romans 12:3
Be honest in your estimate of yourselves.

••• In order to know God better and grow closer to him, we need to be honest with him about everything, including our mistakes and the deep-down feelings in our heart.

PROMISE FROM GOD:

Psalm 37:37
Look at those who are honest and good, for a wonderful future lies before those who love peace.

••• Hope •••

Where does hope come from?

Psalm 39:7
Lord, where do I put my hope? My only hope is in you.

Psalm 71:5
O Lord, you alone are my hope. I've trusted you, O Lord, from childhood.

ooo Those who know Jesus as Savior have lots of hope because he knows their future.

Why should I trust God as my hope?

Hebrews 6:18-19
God has given us both his promise and his oath. These two things are unchangeable because it is impossible for God to lie. Therefore, we who have fled to him for refuge can take new courage, for we can hold on to his promise with confidence. This confidence is like a strong and trustworthy anchor for our souls. It leads us through the curtain of heaven into God's inner sanctuary.

Hebrews 10:23
Without wavering, let us hold tightly to the hope we say we have, for God can be trusted to keep his promise.

1 Peter 1:21
Through Christ you have come to trust in God. And because God raised Christ from the dead and gave him great glory, your faith and hope can be placed confidently in God.

ooo God can't lie, because he *is* truth. God can't break his promises. His word stands forever. God can be trusted to give us hope because he alone defeated death by raising Jesus from the dead.

Where can I go each day to feel hopeful?

Romans 15:4
Such things were written in the Scriptures long ago to teach

us. They give us hope and encouragement as we wait patiently for God's promises.

Psalm 119:43, 74, 81, 114, 147
Do not snatch your word of truth from me, for my only hope is in your laws. . . . May all who fear you find in me a cause for joy, for I have put my hope in your word. . . . I faint with longing for your salvation; but I have put my hope in your word. . . . You are my refuge and my shield; your word is my only source of hope. . . . I rise early, before the sun is up; I cry out for help and put my hope in your words.

Each day we can read God's Word and have our hope strengthened and made new. His Word never fails or changes.

How does hope help me live better today?

Philippians 3:13-14
No, dear brothers and sisters, I am still not all I should be, but I am focusing all my energies on this one thing: Forgetting the past and looking forward to what lies ahead, I strain to reach the end of the race and receive the prize for which God, through Christ Jesus, is calling us up to heaven.

Hope helps us focus on our future, especially our eternal future. Hope also gives us energy to do our best in our daily tasks.

1 John 3:3
All who believe this will keep themselves pure, just as Christ is pure.

Hope helps us keep our life pure before God.

If God's plan for me is the best, can I always be hopeful about the future?

Jeremiah 29:11
"I know the plans I have for you," says the Lord. "They are plans for good and not for disaster, to give you a future and a hope."

Romans 12:12
Be glad for all God is planning for you. Be patient in trouble, and always be prayerful.

Our future will include what God has planned for us. We know that his plans are the best for us, so we can look forward to our future with joyful hope and excitement.

PROMISE FROM GOD:

Psalm 71:5
O Lord, you alone are my hope.

Humility

What is true humility?

Zephaniah 3:12
Those who are left will be the lowly and the humble, for it is they who trust in the name of the Lord.

Humility means not thinking too highly of yourself or thinking that you're better than others.

Matthew 18:4
Anyone who becomes as humble as this little child is the greatest in the Kingdom of Heaven.

ooo Humility is innocent, like a little child who knows he needs help from others.

Titus 3:2
They must not speak evil of anyone, and they must avoid quarreling. Instead, they should be gentle and show true humility to everyone.

ooo Humility means being gentle.

Psalm 51:3-4
I recognize my shameful deeds—they haunt me day and night. Against you, and you alone, have I sinned; I have done what is evil in your sight. You will be proved right in what you say, and your judgment against me is just.

ooo Humility means you're willing to confess and ask forgiveness when you sin.

Proverbs 12:23
Wise people don't make a show of their knowledge, but fools broadcast their folly.

ooo Humble people don't feel like they have to prove themselves to others.

Proverbs 13:10
Pride leads to arguments; those who take advice are wise.

ooo Humility helps us want good advice.

How is Jesus humble?

Zechariah 9:9
Rejoice greatly, O people of Zion! Shout in triumph, O people of Jerusalem! Look, your king is coming to you. He is righteous and victorious, yet he is humble, riding on a donkey—even on a donkey's colt.

ooo Jesus was King of kings, yet he rode on a donkey instead of on a grand horse.

Philippians 2:5-11
Your attitude should be the same that Christ Jesus had. Though he was God, he did not demand and cling to his rights as God. He made himself nothing; he took the humble position of a slave and appeared in human form. And in human form he obediently humbled himself even further by dying a criminal's death on a cross. Because of this, God raised him up to the heights of heaven and gave him a name that is above every other name, so that at the name of Jesus every knee will bow, in heaven and on earth and under the earth, and every tongue will confess that Jesus Christ is Lord, to the glory of God the Father.

ooo Jesus is God, yet he took the lowest position as a servant and suffered death on the cross for us.

Hebrews 2:9
What we do see is Jesus, who "for a little while was made lower than the angels" and now is "crowned with glory and honor" because he suffered death for us. Yes, by God's grace, Jesus tasted death for everyone in all the world.

ooo Jesus had all the glory and honor, but he died so that we could be saved and live forever with him.

Matthew 11:29
Take my yoke upon you. Let me teach you, because I am humble and gentle, and you will find rest for your souls.

ooo Jesus' kind way of treating people and teaching them shows humility.

How can I become humble?

Deuteronomy 8:2-3
Remember how the Lord your God led you through the wilderness for forty years, humbling you and testing you to prove your character, and to find out whether or not you would really obey his commands. Yes, he humbled you by letting you go hungry and then feeding you with manna. . . . He did it to teach you that people need more than bread for their life.

●●● Humility comes when we know that we need God and then watch him meet our needs!

1 Peter 3:8
All of you should be of one mind, full of sympathy toward each other, loving one another with tender hearts and humble minds.

●●● Humility comes from showing love and tender care toward others.

Philippians 2:3
Don't be selfish; don't live to make a good impression on others. Be humble, thinking of others as better than yourself.

●●● Humility means thinking of others as better than yourself.

1 Peter 5:5
You younger men, accept the authority of the elders. And all of you, serve each other in humility, for "God sets himself against the proud, but he shows favor to the humble."

●●● Humility means obeying the authority of those who are over us.

How does God respond to the humble?

Psalm 25:9
He leads the humble in what is right, teaching them his way.

ᴗᴗᴗ God leads and teaches humble people.

Psalm 149:4
The Lord delights in his people; he crowns the humble with salvation.

ᴗᴗᴗ The Lord is very happy with humble people, and he offers them salvation from their sins.

1 Peter 5:6
Humble yourselves under the mighty power of God, and in his good time he will honor you.

ᴗᴗᴗ The Lord honors the humble.

Daniel 10:12
Since the first day you began to pray for understanding and to humble yourself before your God, your request has been heard in heaven. I have come in answer to your prayer.

ᴗᴗᴗ God listens to the prayers of the humble, and he answers them.

Psalm 69:32
The humble will see their God at work and be glad. Let all who seek God's help live in joy.

ᴗᴗᴗ Humility opens our eyes to see God at work in our life.

What is the value of being humble?

2 Samuel 22:28
You rescue those who are humble, but your eyes are on the proud to humiliate them.

••• God rescues the humble.

Proverbs 15:33
Fear of the Lord teaches a person to be wise; humility precedes honor.

Matthew 23:12
Those who exalt themselves will be humbled, and those who humble themselves will be exalted.

••• God honors and takes care of the humble.

Deuteronomy 8:16
He fed you with manna in the wilderness, a food unknown to your ancestors. He did this to humble you and test you for your own good.

••• Humility strengthens our character—it's for our own good.

Proverbs 11:2
Pride leads to disgrace, but with humility comes wisdom.

••• Humility helps us learn to be wise in the things we say and do and think.

How can humility help me admit and confess my sins?

James 4:6-10
He gives us more and more strength to stand against such evil desires. As the Scriptures say, "God sets himself against the proud, but he shows favor to the humble." So humble yourselves before God. Resist the Devil, and he will flee from you. Draw close to God, and God will draw close to you. Wash your hands, you sinners; purify your hearts, you hypocrites. Let there be tears for the wrong things you have done. . . . When

you bow down before the Lord and admit your dependence on him, he will lift you up and give you honor.

Humility is necessary for us to see the sin in our life, admit that we need God, and ask for his forgiveness. A person who is too proud cannot do this.

PROMISE FROM GOD:

Matthew 23:12
Those who exalt themselves will be humbled, and those who humble themselves will be exalted.

Jealousy

Why is jealousy so dangerous?

Proverbs 14:30
A relaxed attitude lengthens life; jealousy rots it away.

Jealousy brings rottenness to our life because it makes us focus on being angry and bitter.

Genesis 13:7
An argument broke out between the herdsmen of Abram and Lot.

Proverbs 27:4
Anger is cruel . . . but who can survive the destructiveness of jealousy?

Jealousy tears families and friends apart. Jealousy drove Lot's herdsmen to fight with his uncle Abram's herdsmen.

What does it mean that God is a "jealous God"?

Exodus 34:14
You must worship no other gods, but only the Lord, for he is a God who is passionate about his relationship with you.

Deuteronomy 5:9
I, the Lord your God, am a jealous God who will not share your affection with any other god!

Deuteronomy 32:21
They have roused my jealousy by worshipping non-gods.

Zechariah 1:14
This is what the Lord Almighty says: My love for Jerusalem and Mount Zion is passionate and strong.

When people give their honor, praise, and love to other things, God is jealous that the honor due him has been given to someone or something else. God is not wrong for being jealous for that reason, because he should be more important to us than anything or anyone else.

What are the results of being jealous?

Proverbs 12:12
Thieves are jealous of each other's loot, while the godly bear their own fruit.

Jealousy easily leads to wanting what others have. Godliness, on the other hand, leads to a life filled with God's goodness, called the fruit of the Spirit.

Genesis 4:4-5
The Lord accepted Abel and his offering, but he did not accept Cain and his offering. This made Cain very angry.

Galatians 5:22-23
When the Holy Spirit controls our lives, he will produce this kind of fruit in us: love, joy, peace, patience, kindness, goodness, faithfulness, gentleness, and self-control.

When we work to grow the character traits that come from the Holy Spirit, we won't get caught up in silly human jealousies and the hard feelings that come from competing with others for honor and popularity.

PROMISE FROM GOD:

Mark 11:24-25
Listen to me! You can pray for anything, and if you believe, you will have it. But when you are praying, first forgive anyone you are holding a grudge against, so that your Father in heaven will forgive your sins, too.

Knowledge/ Learning

Why is learning so important?

Proverbs 1:4
These proverbs will make the simpleminded clever. They will give knowledge and purpose to young people.

Knowledge helps us know what God wants us to do with our life. God will show you what he wants for you as you learn more about him by studying his Word.

Proverbs 2:10
Wisdom will enter your heart, and knowledge will fill you with joy.

●●● Using the wisdom has God given us helps us stay away from many wrong paths.

What is the most important thing to learn?

Proverbs 1:7
Fear of the Lord is the beginning of knowledge. Only fools despise wisdom and discipline.

Proverbs 1:29-31
They hated knowledge and chose not to fear the Lord. They rejected my advice and paid no attention when I corrected them. That is why they must eat the bitter fruit of living their own way.

●●● Learn to fear the Lord. This is not the scared kind of fear, but a fear that shows respect for who God is, why he created you, and what he wants you to do with your knowledge.

How can knowledge be harmful?

Isaiah 47:10-11
You felt secure in all your wickedness. "No one sees me," you said. Your "wisdom" and "knowledge" have caused you to turn away from me and claim, "I am self-sufficient and not accountable to anyone!" So disaster will overtake you.

●●● Knowledge is harmful when it makes us think we don't need God. If we think we can depend on our own smarts, we'll end up very disappointed.

PROMISE FROM GOD:

Proverbs 2:3-5
Cry out for insight and understanding. Search for them. . . . Then you will understand what it means to fear the Lord.

◦ ◦ ◦ Laziness ◦ ◦ ◦

What does the Bible say about laziness?

Proverbs 10:4
Lazy people are soon poor.

Proverbs 13:4
Lazy people want much but get little, but those who work hard will prosper and be satisfied.

Proverbs 15:19
A lazy person has trouble all through life.

Romans 12:11
Never be lazy in your work, but serve the Lord enthusiastically.

◦ ◦ ◦ Laziness brings trouble to a person's life. It's much better to work hard.

Is it a sin to be lazy?

Ezekiel 16:49
Sodom's sins were pride, laziness, and gluttony.

2 Thessalonians 3:11
We hear that some of you are living idle lives, refusing to work and wasting time meddling in other people's business.

1 Timothy 5:13
They are likely to become lazy and spend their time gossiping from house to house, getting into other people's business and saying things they shouldn't.

◦ ◦ ◦ There is a difference between resting and being lazy. The Bible says that laziness is sin, but rest is a reward for working hard. We are responsible for how we spend our time here on earth. God wants us to be hard workers; he doesn't like laziness.

PROMISE FROM GOD:

Proverbs 21:5
Good planning and hard work lead to prosperity.

Loneliness

Why does God let us get lonely?

Genesis 2:18
The Lord God said, "It is not good for the man to be alone. I will make a companion who will help him."

God doesn't want us to be lonely. In fact, God knew Adam needed a companion. Then God created woman.

Romans 8:38-39
I am convinced that nothing can ever separate us from his love. Death can't, and life can't. The angels can't, and the demons can't. Our fears for today, our worries about tomorrow, and even the powers of hell can't keep God's love away. Whether we are high above the sky or in the deepest ocean, nothing in all creation will ever be able to separate us from the love of God that is revealed in Christ Jesus our Lord.

God never intended for us to be alone. He has promised us that he will always be there. Nothing can separate us from him. He wants us to have a relationship with him and with other people.

How can I avoid loneliness?

Romans 12:5
Since we are all one body in Christ, we belong to each other, and each of us needs all the others.

Hebrews 10:25
Let us not neglect our meeting together, as some people do, but encourage and warn each other, especially now that the day of his coming back again is drawing near.

ooo The best way to avoid loneliness is to get together with other believers. All of us need to be involved in a local church.

How can God help me with my loneliness?

Psalm 23:4
Even when I walk through the dark valley of death . . . you are close beside me.

Psalm 139:17
How precious are your thoughts about me, O God!

Isaiah 54:10
The mountains may depart and the hills disappear, but even then I will remain loyal to you.

ooo Recognize that you are not unlovable or deficient just because you are lonely. You have value because God made you, loves you, and promises never to leave you.

Exodus 5:21-22
The foremen said to them, "May the Lord judge you for getting us into this terrible situation. . . ." So Moses went back to the Lord and protested . . . "Why did you send me?"

1 Kings 19:4
He sat down under a solitary broom tree and prayed that he might die.

ooo Don't give up on God when you are lonely. It will cause you to feel sorry for yourself, become discouraged, and give in to temptation.

1 Kings 19:10
I alone am left, and now they are trying to kill me, too.

Matthew 11:2-3
John the Baptist, who was now in prison . . . sent his disciples to ask Jesus, "Are you really the Messiah we've been waiting for, or should we keep looking for someone else?"

1 Peter 4:19
If you are suffering according to God's will, keep on doing what is right, and trust yourself to the God who made you, for he will never fail you.

Sometimes we feel alone in our beliefs in Christ. We can feel better knowing that there are others who love God just as much and that God rewards us for sticking with him when others live differently.

Isaiah 41:10
Don't be afraid, for I am with you. Do not be dismayed, for I am your God. I will strengthen you. I will help you. I will uphold you with my victorious right hand.

John 14:1
Don't be troubled. You trust God, now trust in me.

Loneliness can cause us to be afraid, but God calms our fears.

PROMISE FROM GOD:

Psalm 23:4
Even when I walk through the dark valley of death . . . you are close beside me.

◦◦◦ Love ◦◦◦

Do I have to love other people? What if I don't want to?

John 13:34-35
I am giving you a new commandment: Love each other. Just as I have loved you, you should love each other. Your love for one another will prove to the world that you are my disciples.

1 John 2:9
If anyone says, "I am living in the light," but hates a Christian brother or sister, that person is still living in darkness.

1 Peter 4:8
Love covers a multitude of sins.

1 John 4:12
If we love each other, God lives in us, and his love has been brought to full expression through us.

◦◦◦ Being a Christian comes with certain jobs. One of them is to love others. Our behavior as Christians is proof of whether we love each other, and loving each other is proof that we belong to Christ.

What are some special things that come from a loving relationship?

Proverbs 10:12
Love covers all offenses.

1 Corinthians 13:4-7
Love is patient and kind. Love is not jealous or boastful or proud or rude. Love does not demand its own way. Love is not irritable, and it keeps no record of when it has been wronged. It is never glad about injustice but rejoices whenever the truth

wins out. Love never gives up, never loses faith, is always hopeful, and endures through every circumstance.

●●● There are lots of gifts that come from love, including forgiveness, patience, kindness, seeing the best in a person, loyalty at any cost, and belief in a person no matter what. Love does not include jealousy, envy, pride, a haughty spirit, selfishness, rudeness, demanding your own way, being irritable, or holding grudges.

Does God really love me? How can I know?

John 3:16

God so loved the world that he gave his only Son, so that everyone who believes in him will not perish but have eternal life.

1 John 4:9-10

God showed how much he loved us by sending his only Son into the world so that we might have eternal life through him. This is real love.

●●● We can be totally sure that God loves us, because he sent his Son to suffer in our place and give us eternal life.

Romans 5:5

[God] has given us the Holy Spirit to fill our hearts with his love.

●●● The Holy Spirit's presence in our heart shows us God's love for us.

How should we show our love to God?

Matthew 10:42

If you give even a cup of cold water to one of the least of my followers, you will surely be rewarded.

●●● We show our love for God by showing love to needy people.

John 14:21
Those who obey my commandments are the ones who love me.

ooo We show our love for God by obeying him.

John 21:15-17
Do you love me? . . . Feed my lambs. . . . Take care of my sheep. . . . Feed my sheep.

Hebrews 6:10
[God] will not forget . . . how you have shown your love to him by caring for other Christians.

ooo We show our love for God by guiding and helping other Christians.

Psalm 122:1
I was glad when they said to me, "Let us go to the house of the Lord."

ooo We show our love for God by worshipping him and praising him because of his love for us.

PROMISE FROM GOD:

Romans 8:39
Whether we are high above the sky or in the deepest ocean, nothing in all creation will ever be able to separate us from the love of God that is revealed in Christ Jesus our Lord.

ooo *Lying* ooo

Why do we lie?

Acts 20:30
Even some of you will distort the truth in order to draw a following.

ooo Sometimes we lie to become popular.

Acts 5:2
[Ananias] brought part of the money to the apostles, but he claimed it was the full amount. His wife had agreed to this deception.

ooo Sometimes we lie to make ourselves look good.

Genesis 4:9
The Lord asked Cain, "Where is your brother?". . . "I don't know!" Cain retorted.

ooo Sometimes we think lying will help us avoid punishment.

Why is it so important to tell the truth?

Ephesians 4:25
Put away all falsehood and "tell your neighbor the truth" because we belong to each other.

John 14:6
Jesus told him, "I am the way, the truth, and the life. No one can come to the Father except through me."

ooo God is truth, so lying goes against God. Truth always searches for what is right and good. Lying always wants to cover up the truth.

What does God think about lying?

Proverbs 6:16-17
There are six things the Lord hates—no, seven: . . . haughty eyes, a lying tongue. . . .

Proverbs 12:22
The Lord hates those who don't keep their word, but he delights in those who do.

Romans 1:18
God shows his anger from heaven against all sinful, wicked people who push the truth away from themselves.

God *is* truth, so he must hate lies and lying. He cannot put up with them because they are the opposite of who he is—truth.

How should I feel about lying?

Psalm 119:163
I hate and abhor all falsehood.

Proverbs 13:5
Those who are godly hate lies.

Colossians 3:9
Don't lie to each other, for you have stripped off your old evil nature and all its wicked deeds.

We should hate lies because they are part of the old sinful nature we had before we became Christians.

Can we lie without using words?

Proverbs 10:18
To hide hatred is to be a liar; to slander is to be a fool.

1 John 1:10
If we claim we have not sinned, we are calling God a liar and showing that his word has no place in our hearts.

We lie whenever we try to get away with doing something wrong. These kinds of lies can be to God, others, or even ourselves.

PROMISE FROM GOD:

Proverbs 12:19
Truth stands the test of time; lies are soon exposed.

○ ○ ○ *Maturity* ○ ○ ○

How can we become more mature? Who can help us grow in maturity?

Psalm 32:8
The Lord says, "I will guide you along the best pathway for your life."

Psalm 92:12
The godly will flourish like palm trees.

Psalm 111:10
Reverence for the Lord is the foundation of true wisdom.

Jeremiah 17:8
They are like trees planted along a riverbank, with roots that reach deep into the water.

Ephesians 3:17
I pray that Christ will be more and more at home in your hearts as you trust in him. May your roots go down deep into the soil of God's marvelous love.

Philippians 1:6
I am sure that God, who began the good work within you, will continue his work until it is finally finished.

Colossians 2:7
Let your roots grow down into him and draw up nourishment from him, so you will grow in faith.

●●● Only God, who created us for a purpose and established the rules for how people relate to each other, can help us find the maturity we desire. Reading the Bible and praying to God are the first and most important steps toward maturity.

1 Corinthians 3:1-2
I couldn't talk to you as I would to mature Christians. . . .
I had to feed you with milk and not with solid food.

1 Corinthians 13:11
It's like this: When I was a child, I spoke and thought and reasoned as a child does. But when I grew up, I put away childish things.

Hebrews 6:1
Let us stop going over the basics of Christianity again and again. Let us go on instead and become mature in our understanding.

●●● Spiritual growth is like physical growth—we start small and then grow up one day at a time.

What might keep us from maturing as we want? What must we stay away from?

Isaiah 59:2
There is a problem—your sins have cut you off from God.

2 Timothy 2:4
As Christ's soldier, do not let yourself become tied up in the affairs of this life.

●●● There are roadblocks to maturing the way we want. Sin is one. Getting distracted by being too busy is another. Beware of these roadblocks, because they will keep you from spiritual maturity.

PROMISE FROM GOD:

Philippians 4:13
I can do everything with the help of Christ who gives me the strength I need.

Miracles

What are miracles?

Isaiah 41:19-20
I will plant trees—cedar, acacia, myrtle, olive, cypress, fir, and pine—on barren land. Everyone will see this miracle and understand that it is the Lord, the Holy One of Israel, who did it.

Miracles are things that only God can do that help us know him and see him working in our life.

How does God use miracles?

2 Kings 17:36
Worship only the Lord, who brought you out of Egypt with such mighty miracles and power. You must worship him and bow before him; offer sacrifices to him alone.

Daniel 6:27
He rescues and saves his people; he performs miraculous signs and wonders in the heavens and on earth. He has rescued Daniel from the power of the lions.

Micah 7:15
"Yes," says the Lord, "I will do mighty miracles for you, like those I did when I rescued you from slavery in Egypt."

God uses miracles to rescue us.

Exodus 10:1
Then the Lord said to Moses, "Return to Pharaoh and again make your demands. I have made him and his officials stubborn so I can continue to display my power by performing miraculous signs among them."

ooo God uses miracles to demonstrate his power.

Matthew 8:3
Jesus touched him. "I want to [make you well]," he said. "Be healed!" And instantly the leprosy disappeared.

ooo God uses miracles to show his love for us.

Matthew 14:14
A vast crowd was there as he stepped from the boat, and he had compassion on them and healed their sick.

ooo God uses miracles to show his compassion for us.

What should we do when God performs miracles in our life?

Luke 19:37
As they reached the place where the road started down from the Mount of Olives, all of his followers began to shout and sing as they walked along, praising God for all the wonderful miracles they had seen.

ooo We should praise and thank him.

Psalm 9:1
I will thank you, Lord, with all my heart; I will tell of all the marvelous things you have done.

ooo We can show our thanks by telling others what God has done for us.

PROMISE FROM GOD:

Jeremiah 32:18-19
You are the great and powerful God, the Lord Almighty. You have all wisdom and do great and mighty miracles.

Mistakes

What does the Bible have to say about mistakes?

Genesis 3:12-13
"Yes," Adam admitted, "but it was the woman you gave me who brought me the fruit." . . . "The serpent tricked me," she replied.

Both Adam and Eve refused to take the blame for their sin. Instead, Adam blamed Eve and Eve blamed the snake.

Judges 16:17, 21, 28
Finally, Samson told her his secret. . . . The Philistines captured him and gouged out his eyes. . . . Then Samson prayed to the Lord, "Sovereign Lord, remember me again."

Even though Samson made many foolish mistakes, God still mightily used him.

James 3:2
We all make many mistakes, but those who control their tongues can also control themselves in every other way.

One of the most common mistakes is saying something we shouldn't say.

Jonah 1:3
Jonah got up and went in the opposite direction in order to get away from the Lord.

••• The worst mistake we can make is running from God.

Exodus 2:12
After looking around to make sure no one was watching, Moses killed the Egyptian and buried him in the sand.

••• Even Moses made immature and terrible mistakes.

Matthew 26:74
Peter said, "I swear by God, I don't know the man."

••• Christ forgave Peter even after Peter's most painful mistake of pretending he didn't even know Jesus.

PROMISE FROM GOD:

Philippians 3:13-14
No, dear brothers and sisters, I am still not all I should be, but I am focusing all my energies on this one thing: Forgetting the past and looking forward to what lies ahead, I strain to reach the end of the race and receive the prize for which God, through Christ Jesus, is calling us up to heaven.

••• *Modesty* •••

Why is modesty important?

1 Peter 2:12
Be careful how you live among your unbelieving neighbors. Even if they accuse you of doing wrong, they will see your honorable behavior, and they will believe and give honor to God when he comes to judge the world.

1 Peter 3:1-2
In the same way, you wives must accept the authority of your husbands, even those who refuse to accept the Good News. Your

godly lives will speak to them better than any words. They will be won over by watching your pure, godly behavior.

Godly modesty means setting an example of doing right, which no one can criticize. Modesty can bring people to God—even people who might have turned away from him in the past.

How can I be modest in my appearance?

1 Timothy 2:9
I want women to be modest in their appearance. They should wear decent and appropriate clothing and not draw attention to themselves.

1 Corinthians 6:19
Don't you know that your body is the temple of the Holy Spirit, who lives in you and was given to you by God? You do not belong to yourself.

1 Peter 3:3-4
Don't be concerned about the outward beauty that depends on fancy hairstyles, expensive jewelry, or beautiful clothes. You should be known for the beauty that comes from within, the unfading beauty of a gentle and quiet spirit, which is so precious to God.

Modesty focuses on inner beauty—who we are—for that kind of beauty stays strong and youthful long after our body turns old and frail.

How can I be modest in my actions?

Romans 13:13
We should be decent and true in everything we do, so that everyone can approve of our behavior. Don't participate in wild

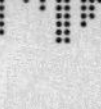

parties and getting drunk, or in adultery and immoral living, or in fighting and jealousy.

Ephesians 5:8
Though your hearts were once full of darkness, now you are full of light from the Lord, and your behavior should show it!

Titus 2:12
We are instructed to turn from godless living and sinful pleasures. We should live in this evil world with self-control, right conduct, and devotion to God.

We can show modesty by living with self-control, avoiding inappropriate behavior, keeping ourselves close to God, and shining Christ's light in a dark world.

PROMISE FROM GOD:

1 Peter 2:12
Be careful how you live among your unbelieving neighbors. Even if they accuse you of doing wrong, they will see your honorable behavior, and they will believe and give honor to God when he comes to judge the world.

Money

What is a good attitude to have toward money?

Psalm 23:1
The Lord is my shepherd; I have everything I need.

Matthew 6:24
No one can serve two masters. . . . You cannot serve both God and money.

••• Money cannot satisfy our deepest needs. We need to keep reminding ourselves that God must be first in our lives.

Psalm 119:36
Give me an eagerness for your decrees; do not inflict me with love for money!

1 Timothy 6:10
The love of money is at the root of all kinds of evil.

Hebrews 13:5
Stay away from the love of money; be satisfied with what you have. For God has said, "I will never fail you. I will never forsake you."

••• *Money* is not the root of all kinds of evil—the *love* of it is!

Proverbs 11:28
Trust in your money and down you go!

Isaiah 55:2
Why spend your money on food that does not give you strength? . . . Listen, and I will tell you where to get food that is good for the soul!

••• Too often we buy things because we think those things will make us happier. The Bible shows the way to get deep and lasting happiness that always satisfies.

Proverbs 19:1
It is better to be poor and honest than to be a fool and dishonest.

Mark 8:36
How do you benefit if you gain the whole world but lose your own soul in the process?

●●● No amount of money is worth getting dishonestly. Taking advantage of others to make money is stealing. Those who do this lose far more than they could ever gain.

Philippians 4:11-12
I have learned how to get along happily whether I have much or little. . . . I have learned the secret of living in every situation.

Philippians 4:19
This same God who takes care of me will supply all your needs from his glorious riches.

●●● The Bible promises that God will supply all of our needs. The problem comes when our definition of "need" is different from God's. The first thing we must do is study God's Word to discover what he says we need for a fulfilling life.

Mark 12:43
He called his disciples to him and said, "I assure you, this poor widow has given more than all the others have given."

1 John 3:17
If anyone has enough money to live well and sees a brother or sister in need and refuses to help—how can God's love be in that person?

●●● Giving generously might be the best way to keep us from loving our money. When we see what giving does for other people, we feel happy knowing that lots of money and "stuff" can't give us real happiness that lasts. This kind of giving shows God's love.

Proverbs 3:9-10
Honor the Lord with your wealth and with the best part of everything your land produces. Then he will fill your barns with grain.

Malachi 3:10
"Bring all the tithes into the storehouse. . . . If you do," says the Lord Almighty, "I will open the windows of heaven for you."

Instead of thinking money is ours, to use however we want, we should think of it as God's, to use as *he* wishes. Giving God the first part of everything we earn will help us keep this attitude.

2 Corinthians 9:6
The one who plants generously will get a generous crop.

Proverbs 21:20
Fools spend whatever they get.

Proverbs 28:19
Hard workers have plenty of food.

Matthew 25:14
He called together his servants and gave them money to invest for him while he was gone.

1 Corinthians 4:12
We have worked wearily with our own hands to earn our living.

Luke 6:38
If you give, you will receive.

God commands us to be smart in earning, spending, and saving our money. He understands the importance of earning the money we need. But he also expects us to use our money generously to help others.

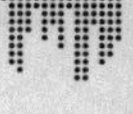

Why do we always seem to want more?

Ecclesiastes 10:19
A party gives laughter, and wine gives happiness, and money gives everything!

ooo Money can get us many things in the world. That's why we want it.

Mark 10:22
At this, the man's face fell, and he went sadly away because he had many possessions.

ooo We want more money because we think money and wealth will bring us happiness. How much more happy and useful we could be if we set our mind to earning treasure in heaven!

Why don't I ever seem to have enough?

Isaiah 55:2
Why spend your money on food that does not give you strength?

ooo We don't have enough when we foolishly waste our money on unimportant things.

Haggai 1:4
Why are you living in luxurious houses while my house lies in ruins?

ooo We don't have enough when we don't manage our money according to God's priorities.

Luke 12:15
Don't be greedy for what you don't have. Real life is not measured by how much we own.

●●● If we depend on our wealth to bring security, there will never be enough.

Is debt a sin?

Proverbs 22:7
Just as the rich rule the poor, so the borrower is servant to the lender.

●●● It is wise to avoid borrowing money.

Proverbs 6:1, 3
If you co-sign a loan for a friend or guarantee the debt of someone you hardly know . . . get out of it if you possibly can!

●●● Debt is a dangerous thing. We should avoid it whenever possible.

Romans 13:8
Pay all your debts.

●●● Failing to repay a debt is clearly sinful.

PROMISE FROM GOD:

Matthew 6:31-33
Don't worry about having enough food or drink or clothing. Why be like the pagans who are so deeply concerned about these things? Your heavenly Father already knows all your needs, and he will give you all you need from day to day if you live for him and make the Kingdom of God your primary concern.

○○○ Motives ○○○

Does God care about our motives?

1 Chronicles 29:17
I know, my God, that you examine our hearts and rejoice when you find integrity there. You know I have done all this with good motives, and I have watched your people offer their gifts willingly and joyously.

Proverbs 20:27
The Lord's searchlight penetrates the human spirit, exposing every hidden motive.

Proverbs 21:27
God loathes the sacrifice of an evil person, especially when it is brought with ulterior motives.

○○○ Our motives are very important to God.

1 Samuel 16:7
But the Lord said to Samuel, "Don't judge by his appearance or height, for I have rejected him. The Lord doesn't make decisions the way you do! People judge by outward appearance, but the Lord looks at a person's thoughts and intentions."

○○○ God puts more importance on our motives than on our appearance or outward actions.

James 4:3
When you do ask, you don't get it because your whole motive is wrong—you want only what will give you pleasure.

○○○ Wrong motives can hinder our prayers.

Philippians 1:17-18
Those others do not have pure motives as they preach about Christ. They preach with selfish ambition, not sincerely,

intending to make my chains more painful to me. But whether or not their motives are pure, the fact remains that the message about Christ is being preached, so I rejoice. And I will continue to rejoice.

••• Even when our motives are wrong, God can use us for good.

How can I have motives that please God?

1 Chronicles 28:9-10
Solomon, my son, get to know the God of your ancestors. Worship and serve him with your whole heart and with a willing mind. For the Lord sees every heart and understands and knows every plan and thought. If you seek him, you will find him. But if you forsake him, he will reject you forever. So take this seriously.

••• Worshipping and serving God with our whole heart and mind can give us right motives.

Psalm 19:14
May the words of my mouth and the thoughts of my heart be pleasing to you, O Lord, my rock and my redeemer.

••• Ask God to give you motives that please him.

Psalm 26:2
Put me on trial, Lord, and cross-examine me. Test my motives and affections.

Proverbs 17:3
Fire tests the purity of silver and gold, but the Lord tests the heart.

••• God will test our motives, giving us an opportunity to grow.

PROMISE FROM GOD:

Ezekiel 36:26
I will give you a new heart with new and right desires, and I will put a new spirit in you. I will take out your stony heart of sin and give you a new, obedient heart.

Music

Does God like music?

2 Chronicles 5:13-14
The trumpeters and singers performed together in unison to praise and give thanks to the Lord. Accompanied by trumpets, cymbals, and other instruments, they raised their voices and praised the Lord with these words: "He is so good! His faithful love endures forever!" At that moment a cloud filled the Temple of the Lord. The priests could not continue their work because the glorious presence of the Lord filled the Temple of God.

God likes music—he came with all his power and entered the Temple during a time of musical worship.

Zephaniah 3:17
The Lord your God has arrived to live among you. . . . He will exult over you by singing a happy song.

God created music—he himself is the singer!

Psalm 147:1
How good it is to sing praises to our God! How delightful and how right!

God delights when we use music to praise him.

What role does music have in worship?

2 Chronicles 23:13
The officers and trumpeters were surrounding him, and people from all over the land were rejoicing and blowing trumpets. Singers with musical instruments were leading the people in a great celebration.

Throughout God's Word, people used music to worship the Lord.

Psalm 81:2-4
Sing! Beat the tambourine. Play the sweet lyre and the harp. Sound the trumpet for a sacred feast when the moon is new, when the moon is full. For this is required by the laws of Israel; it is a law of the God of Jacob.

David saw music as a required form of worship.

Are there types of music that we should stay away from?

Philippians 4:8
Now, dear brothers and sisters, let me say one more thing as I close this letter. Fix your thoughts on what is true and honorable and right. Think about things that are pure and lovely and admirable. Think about things that are excellent and worthy of praise.

As Christians, we should protect our mind from things that are not pure. We should avoid music that leads us to think about untrue, dishonorable, or impure things.

PROMISE FROM GOD:

Isaiah 51:11
Those who have been ransomed by the Lord will return

to Jerusalem, singing songs of everlasting joy. Sorrow and mourning will disappear, and they will be overcome with joy and gladness.

••• Obedience •••

Since Jesus forgives me, do I still need to obey him?

Deuteronomy 10:12-13
Now, Israel, what does the Lord your God require of you? He requires you to fear him, to live according to his will, to love and worship him with all your heart and soul, and to obey the Lord's commands and laws that I am giving you today for your own good.

Philippians 2:12
Dearest friends, you were always so careful to follow my instructions when I was with you. And now that I am away you must be even more careful to put into action God's saving work in your lives, obeying God with deep reverence and fear.

••• Obedience is putting into action God's saving work in our life.

Jeremiah 7:23
Obey me, and I will be your God, and you will be my people. Only do as I say, and all will be well!

••• Obedience to God is a necessary part of our relationship with him.

Hebrews 11:8
It was by faith that Abraham obeyed.

ooo Obedience is an act of faith. Sometimes it's hard, but we know that God *always* blesses us when we obey.

Romans 1:5
Through Christ, God has given us the privilege and authority to tell Gentiles everywhere what God has done for them, so that they will believe and obey him, bringing glory to his name.

Romans 6:17
Thank God! Once you were slaves of sin, but now you have obeyed with all your heart the new teaching God has given you.

ooo Putting our trust in God for salvation through Christ is the same as obeying his message of the Good News.

Titus 1:16
Such people claim they know God, but they deny him by the way they live. They are despicable and disobedient, worthless for doing anything good.

ooo If we keep being disobedient to God, no one will believe that we know him.

Leviticus 9:6
Moses told them, "When you have followed these instructions from the Lord, the glorious presence of the Lord will appear to you."

In what ways does God want us to obey him?

Genesis 6:22
Noah did everything exactly as God had commanded him.

Deuteronomy 5:32
You must obey all the commands of the Lord your God, following his instructions in every detail.

●●● God wants us to do everything he commands us to do.

1 Samuel 15:22
Samuel replied, "What is more pleasing to the Lord: your burnt offerings and sacrifices or your obedience to his voice? Obedience is far better than sacrifice. Listening to him is much better than offering the fat of rams.

●●● Obedience to God means listening to what he says.

Exodus 12:28
The people of Israel did just as the Lord had commanded through Moses and Aaron.

Romans 13:1
Obey the government, for God is the one who put it there. All governments have been placed in power by God.

Hebrews 13:17
Obey your spiritual leaders and do what they say.

●●● God shows us through human authorities what he wants us to do.

Exodus 1:17
Because the midwives feared God, they refused to obey the king and allowed the boys to live, too.

Acts 4:19-20
Peter and John replied, "Do you think God wants us to obey you rather than him? We cannot stop telling about the wonderful things we have seen and heard."

Acts 5:29
Peter and the apostles replied, "We must obey God rather than human authority."

●●● We must obey God over human authorities.

PROMISE FROM GOD:

James 1:25

If you keep looking steadily into God's perfect law—the law that sets you free—and if you do what it says and don't forget what you heard, then God will bless you for doing it.

Parents

How should we treat our parents?

Exodus 20:12

Honor your father and mother. Then you will live a long, full life in the land the Lord your God will give you.

Mark 7:12-13

You let them disregard their needy parents. As such, you break the law of God in order to protect your own tradition. And this is only one example. There are many, many others.

Ephesians 6:1

Children, obey your parents because you belong to the Lord, for this is the right thing to do.

Even if we disagree with our parents, we must still show them honor, respect, and obedience.

PROMISE FROM GOD:

Ephesians 6:3

This is the promise: If you honor your father and mother, "you will live a long life, full of blessing."

○○○ Patience ○○○

How can I grow in patience?

Psalm 40:1
I waited patiently for the Lord to help me, and he turned to me and heard my cry.

○○○ We must pray and wait patiently for God to do his work in us.

Habakkuk 2:3
If it seems slow, wait patiently, for it will surely take place. It will not be delayed.

○○○ We develop patience as we learn to live for God.

Galatians 5:22
When the Holy Spirit controls our lives, he will produce this kind of fruit in us: love, joy, peace, patience.

○○○ Patience comes from the Holy Spirit working in our heart.

1 Corinthians 13:4
Love is patient and kind.

○○○ Patience shows love.

Romans 8:25
If we look forward to something we don't have yet, we must wait patiently and confidently.

○○○ Patience comes through a believer's hope in God's wonderful plan for eternity.

PROMISE FROM GOD:

Lamentations 3:25
The Lord is wonderfully good to those who wait for him and seek him.

Peer Pressure

Is all peer pressure bad?

James 4:17
Remember, it is sin to know what you ought to do and then not do it.

Good peer pressure will help you obey God's Word.

How do I tell the difference between good and bad peer pressure?

Matthew 7:20
Yes, the way to identify a tree or a person is by the kind of fruit that is produced.

Good peer pressure will encourage you toward living a more godly life, while bad peer pressure will lead you away from godly living.

When is peer pressure bad?

Romans 6:12
Do not let sin control the way you live; do not give in to its lustful desires.

When peer pressure involves sin of any kind, it isn't good.

1 Samuel 15:24
Then Saul finally admitted, "Yes, I have sinned. I have disobeyed your instructions and the Lord's command, for I was afraid of the people and did what they demanded."

Exodus 23:2
Do not join a crowd that intends to do evil.

3 John 1:11
Dear friend, don't let this bad example influence you. Follow only what is good.

Peer pressure is harmful when it makes you want to please people more than God or when it causes you to follow the bad example of others.

What is a danger of peer pressure?

Proverbs 25:26
If the godly compromise with the wicked, it is like polluting a fountain or muddying a spring.

Exodus 34:12
Be very careful never to make treaties with the people in the land where you are going. If you do, you soon will be following their evil ways.

Hanging out with the wrong kinds of people can lead us to sin.

What should I do when I'm tempted to give in to peer pressure?

1 Corinthians 10:13
Remember that the temptations that come into your life are no different from what others experience. And God is faithful. He will keep the temptation from becoming so strong that

you can't stand up against it. When you are tempted, he will show you a way out so that you will not give in to it.

1 Corinthians 16:13
Be on guard. Stand true to what you believe. Be courageous. Be strong.

Ephesians 6:11
Put on all of God's armor so that you will be able to stand firm against all strategies and tricks of the Devil.

●●● It's never okay to please others when it means doing something the Bible says is wrong.

How can we resist peer pressure?

Luke 20:21
They said, "Teacher, we know that you speak and teach what is right and are not influenced by what others think. You sincerely teach the ways of God."

●●● It is easier to say no to bad influences when you have been spending time in God's Word.

PROMISE FROM GOD:

1 Corinthians 10:13
Remember that the temptations that come into your life are no different from what others experience. And God is faithful. He will keep the temptation from becoming so strong that you can't stand up against it. When you are tempted, he will show you a way out so that you will not give in to it.

◦◦◦ Persecution ◦◦◦

Why do Christians experience persecution?

John 15:20-21
Since they persecuted me, naturally they will persecute you. And if they had listened to me, they would listen to you! The people of the world will hate you because you belong to me.

Galatians 5:11
The fact that I am still being persecuted proves that I am still preaching salvation.

◦◦◦ Many people don't want good and right to win over evil. Those who oppose God and what is good will persecute Christians. In many cases, persecution is a sign that you are making a real difference for Christ.

If God has a plan for my life, what is the purpose of persecution?

2 Thessalonians 1:5
God will use this persecution to show his justice. For he will make you worthy of his Kingdom, for which you are suffering.

◦◦◦ Persecution defines who we are going to be in Christ. We grow as we respond to persecution in a godly way.

When we experience persecution, what are we supposed to do?

Matthew 5:44
Love your enemies! Pray for those who persecute you!

Romans 12:14
If people persecute you because you are a Christian, don't curse them; pray that God will bless them.

We are to pray that God will bless those who persecute us, for it may be through our response to persecution that God will soften someone else's hard heart.

Revelation 14:12
Let this encourage God's holy people to endure persecution patiently and remain firm to the end, obeying his commands and trusting in Jesus.

Matthew 27:12
When the leading priests and other leaders made their accusations against him, Jesus remained silent.

We should stay obedient to God and be patient through the persecution, just as Jesus did when he was persecuted.

PROMISE FROM GOD:

Matthew 5:11-12
God blesses you when you are mocked and persecuted and lied about because you are my followers. Be happy about it! Be very glad! For a great reward awaits you in heaven.

Planning

Why should I plan ahead?

Genesis 41:28, 33, 36
This will happen just as I have described it, for God has shown you what he is about to do. . . . My suggestion is that you find the wisest man in Egypt and put him in charge of a nationwide program. . . . That way there will be enough to eat when the seven years of famine come. Otherwise disaster will surely strike the land, and all the people will die.

Proverbs 13:16
Wise people think before they act; fools don't and even brag about it!

Proverbs 14:8
The wise look ahead to see what is coming, but fools deceive themselves.

Proverbs 22:3
A prudent person foresees the danger ahead and takes precautions; the simpleton goes blindly on and suffers the consequences.

••• Planning and thinking ahead will help us be ready for danger ahead so that we don't face disastrous consequences.

Proverbs 20:4
If you are too lazy to plow in the right season, you will have no food at the harvest.

Luke 14:28
Don't begin until you count the cost. For who would begin construction of a building without first getting estimates and then checking to see if there is enough money to pay the bills?

••• Planning is an important part of living.

How do I go about planning ahead?

Exodus 25:40
Be sure that you make everything according to the pattern I have shown you here on the mountain.

Genesis 11:4
Let's build a great city with a tower that reaches to the skies—a monument to our greatness! This will bring us together and keep us from scattering all over the world.

Don't make plans that conflict with God's standards.

1 Chronicles 28:19
"Every part of this plan," David told Solomon, "was given to me in writing from the hand of the Lord."

Proverbs 3:5-6
Trust in the Lord with all your heart; do not depend on your own understanding. Seek his will in all you do, and he will direct your paths.

As we get to know God, he will guide us in making our plans.

Isaiah 14:26-27
I have a plan for the whole earth, for my mighty power reaches throughout the world. The Lord Almighty has spoken—who can change his plans? When his hand moves, who can stop him?

Romans 8:28
We know that God causes everything to work together for the good of those who love God and are called according to his purpose for them.

Proverbs 19:21
You can make many plans, but the Lord's purpose will prevail.

God will work through our plans, and in spite of them, to do his will.

PROMISE FROM GOD:

Ephesians 1:9-10
God's secret plan has now been revealed to us; it is a plan centered on Christ, designed long ago according to his good pleasure. And this is his plan: At the right time he will bring everything together under the authority of Christ—everything in heaven and on earth.

Poor

Doesn't God care that I'm poor? I feel so lonely because so many others seem to have all they need while I'm struggling.

Isaiah 25:4
To the poor, O Lord, you are a refuge from the storm . . . a shelter from the rain and the heat.

Matthew 8:20
Jesus said, "Foxes have dens to live in, and birds have nests, but I, the Son of Man, have no home of my own, not even a place to lay my head."

Romans 8:35, 37
Does it mean [God] no longer loves us if we have trouble or calamity, or are persecuted, or are hungry or cold or in danger or threatened with death? . . . No . . . overwhelming victory is ours through Christ, who loved us.

God knows what poverty is like—Christ himself was homeless! God cares and will be our refuge, even as we experience poverty.

Does God really care about the poor?

Psalm 35:10
Who else rescues the weak and helpless from the strong? Who else protects the poor and needy from those who want to rob them?

Psalm 40:17
I am poor and needy, but the Lord is thinking about me right now.

Psalm 72:12
He will rescue the poor when they cry to him; he will help the oppressed, who have no one to defend them.

Psalm 102:17
He will listen to the prayers of the destitute. He will not reject their pleas.

Psalm 113:6-8
Far below him are the heavens and the earth. He stoops to look, and he lifts the poor from the dirt and the needy from the garbage dump. He sets them among princes.

God cares deeply for the poor, and he commands all believers to care for them too.

What is my responsibility to the poor?

Leviticus 25:39
If any of your Israelite relatives go bankrupt and sell themselves to you, do not treat them as slaves.

Proverbs 19:17
If you help the poor, you are lending to the Lord—and he will repay you!

Proverbs 22:9
Blessed are those who are generous, because they feed the poor.

Isaiah 58:10
Feed the hungry and help those in trouble. Then your light will shine out from the darkness, and the darkness around you will be as bright as day.

Matthew 7:12
Do for others what you would like them to do for you.

James 2:9
If you pay special attention to the rich, you are committing a sin.

God has compassion for the poor, so if we want to be godly, we must have compassion for the poor. Helping the poor is a privilege that can bring us great joy.

PROMISE FROM GOD:

2 Corinthians 8:9
You know how full of love and kindness our Lord Jesus Christ was. Though he was very rich, yet for your sakes he became poor, so that by his poverty he could make you rich.

Popularity

What does the Bible say about being popular?

Galatians 1:10
Obviously, I'm not trying to be a people pleaser! No, I am trying to please God. If I were still trying to please people, I would not be Christ's servant.

The Bible cautions us about our motives for wanting to be popular. If we are trying to please people more than God, then we are not serving him, and we have wrong priorities.

How should we respond to someone else's popularity?

John 3:26-27, 30
John's disciples came to him and said, "Teacher, the man you met on the other side of the Jordan River, the one you said was

the Messiah, is also baptizing people. And everybody is going over there instead of coming here to us." John replied, "God in heaven appoints each person's work. . . . He must become greater and greater, and I must become less and less."

●●● Popularity can lead to pride. John the Baptist understood that he had a job to do for God—he did not worry about his own popularity. By contrast, his disciples wrongly became jealous over who was baptizing more people.

What are some of the traps of wanting to be popular?

Esther 3:2
All the king's officials would bow down before Haman to show him respect whenever he passed by, for so the king had commanded. But Mordecai refused to bow down or show him respect.

●●● We should avoid popularity when it causes us to disown or disobey God.

John 12:43
They loved human praise more than the praise of God.

●●● We should avoid popularity when we recognize that our love for popularity is greater than our love for God.

PROMISE FROM GOD:

Matthew 23:12
Those who exalt themselves will be humbled, and those who humble themselves will be exalted.

◦◦◦ Prayer ◦◦◦

What is prayer?

2 Chronicles 7:14
If my people who are called by my name will humble themselves and pray and seek my face and turn from their wicked ways, I will hear from heaven.

◦◦◦ Prayer is an act of humble worship; through prayer we seek God with all our heart.

Psalm 38:18
I confess my sins; I am deeply sorry for what I have done.

◦◦◦ Prayer often begins by confessing our sins.

1 Samuel 14:36
The priest said, "Let's ask God first."

2 Samuel 5:19
David asked the Lord, "Should I go out to fight the Philistines?"

◦◦◦ Prayer is asking God for guidance and waiting for his direction and leading.

Mark 1:35
The next morning Jesus awoke long before daybreak and went out alone into the wilderness to pray.

◦◦◦ Prayer is part of a growing relationship with our heavenly Father, who makes his own love and power available to us.

Psalm 9:1-2
I will thank you, Lord, with all my heart. . . . I will sing praises to your name, O Most High.

○○○ Through prayer we praise our mighty God.

Does the Bible teach a "right" way to pray?

Nehemiah 1:4
For days I mourned, fasted, and prayed to the God of heaven.

○○○ Throughout the Bible, prayer includes praise, confession, and thanksgiving, as well as requests.

Matthew 6:9
Pray like this.

○○○ Jesus taught his disciples that true prayer is the result of an intimate relationship with the Father and includes a dependency for daily needs, commitment to obedience, and forgiveness of sin.

Luke 18:1
One day Jesus told his disciples a story to illustrate their need for constant prayer and to show them that they must never give up.

○○○ We must keep praying throughout the day and never give up; God will answer.

Does God always answer prayer?

James 5:16
Confess your sins to each other and pray for each other so that you may be healed. The earnest prayer of a righteous person has great power and wonderful results.

1 John 5:14
We can be confident that he will listen to us whenever we ask him for anything in line with his will.

••• We can be confident that God will respond to our prayer when we don't demand our own way.

2 Corinthians 12:8-9
Three different times I begged the Lord to take it away. Each time he said, "My power works best in your weakness."

••• Sometimes, like Paul, we find that God answers prayer by not giving us what we ask for. Instead, he gives us something better.

Exodus 14:15
The Lord said to Moses, "Why are you crying out to me? Tell the people to get moving!"

••• Our prayer must include a willingness to obey with our actions.

PROMISE FROM GOD:

1 Peter 3:12
The eyes of the Lord watch over those who do right, and his ears are open to their prayers.

••• Priorities •••

What should be my highest priority?

Mark 12:29-30
Jesus replied, "The most important commandment is this: 'Hear, O Israel! The Lord our God is the one and only Lord. And you must love the Lord your God with all your heart, all your soul, all your mind, and all your strength.' "

••• The most important priority is to love God.

How can I develop the right priorities?

Proverbs 3:5-6
Trust in the Lord with all your heart; do not depend on your own understanding. Seek his will in all you do, and he will direct your paths.

1 Kings 3:9
Give me an understanding mind so that I can govern your people well and know the difference between right and wrong. For who by himself is able to govern this great nation of yours?

1 Samuel 14:36
Then Saul said, "Let's chase the Philistines all night and destroy every last one of them." His men replied, "We'll do whatever you think is best." But the priest said, "Let's ask God first."

Matthew 8:22
Jesus told him, "Follow me now! Let those who are spiritually dead care for their own dead."

••• Seeking God and doing his will should be our first priority. It will help put all of our other priorities in order.

What are some of the benefits of living by right priorities, and what are the dangers of living by wrong priorities?

Psalm 128:1-4
How happy are those who fear the Lord—all who follow his ways! You will enjoy the fruit of your labor. How happy you will be! How rich your life! Your wife will be like a fruitful vine, flourishing within your home. And look at all those children! There they sit around your table as vigorous and healthy as young olive trees. That is the Lord's reward for those who fear him.

Proverbs 14:26
Those who fear the Lord are secure; he will be a place of refuge for their children.

ooo Right priorities bring true happiness, joy, delight, and a full life.

Psalm 127:1-2
Unless the Lord builds a house, the work of the builders is useless. Unless the Lord protects a city, guarding it with sentries will do no good. It is useless for you to work so hard from early morning until late at night, anxiously working for food to eat; for God gives rest to his loved ones.

ooo Wrong priorities can lead to wasting our lives with worry and useless activities.

What should be my priority about winning?

Romans 12:3
As God's messenger, I give each of you this warning: Be honest in your estimate of yourselves, measuring your value by how much faith God has given you.

Mark 10:31
Many who seem to be important now will be the least important then, and those who are considered least here will be the greatest then.

ooo Living by God's plan should be a higher priority than personal achievement.

How do I know if my priorities are right?

Proverbs 3:5-6
Trust in the Lord with all your heart; do not depend on your own understanding. Seek his will in all you do, and he will direct your paths.

Haggai 1:9
You hoped for rich harvests, but they were poor. And when you brought your harvest home, I blew it away. Why? Because my house lies in ruins, says the Lord Almighty, while you are all busy building your own fine houses.

Luke 12:34
Wherever your treasure is, there your heart and thoughts will also be.

Priorities show how much we love God. We focus most on what or whom we love most.

PROMISE FROM GOD:

Proverbs 3:6
Seek his will in all you do, and he will direct your paths.

Procrastination

Why do I procrastinate?

Proverbs 6:10-11
A little extra sleep, a little more slumber, a little folding of the hands to rest—and poverty will pounce on you like a bandit.

Procrastination is often a form of laziness and leads to disaster.

Joshua 18:3
How long are you going to wait before taking possession of the remaining land?

Procrastination is sometimes a form of disobedience.

Matthew 25:25
I was afraid I would lose your money, so I hid it in the earth.

••• Procrastination can keep us fearful of failure and cause us to waste what we have.

Ephesians 5:16
Make the most of every opportunity for doing good in these evil days.

••• Time is a gift from God and must not be wasted.

Matthew 25:13
Stay awake and be prepared, because you do not know the day or hour of my return.

••• Failure to be prepared for the coming of Christ is the most costly form of spiritual procrastination.

PROMISE FROM GOD:

Matthew 25:29
To those who use well what they are given, even more will be given, and they will have an abundance. But from those who are unfaithful, even what little they have will be taken away.

••• Profanity •••

They're just words. Why is profanity such a big deal?

Philippians 4:8
Fix your thoughts on what is true and honorable and right. Think about things that are pure and lovely.

Our mind is to be filled not with the profane, but with the holy.

Exodus 20:7
Do not misuse the name of the Lord your God.

To use the name of God wrongly is to violate God's standard for holiness.

Exodus 21:17
Anyone who curses father or mother must be put to death.

To curse one's parents is as serious an offense as doing them physical harm.

Ephesians 5:4
Obscene stories, foolish talk, and coarse jokes—these are not for you. Instead, let there be thankfulness to God.

Foul language has no part in a believer's vocabulary.

PROMISE FROM GOD:

James 3:2
Those who control their tongues can also control themselves in every other way.

Quitting

How can I keep going when I feel like quitting?

Nehemiah 4:2-3
What does this bunch of poor, feeble Jews think they are doing? . . . That stone wall would collapse if even a fox walked along the top of it!

Nehemiah kept his eyes on the goal and his call, no matter how tough things got.

Acts 20:22
Now I am going to Jerusalem, drawn there irresistibly by the Holy Spirit, not knowing what awaits me.

Paul faced huge hardships, yet he finished his work for God.

2 Corinthians 4:8
We are pressed on every side by troubles, but we are not crushed and broken. We are perplexed, but we don't give up and quit.

Even when believers suffer, God can give them strength to keep going.

2 Timothy 4:7
I have fought a good fight, I have finished the race, and I have remained faithful.

Matthew 10:22
Those who endure to the end will be saved.

Galatians 6:9
Don't get tired of doing what is good. Don't get discouraged and give up, for we will reap a harvest of blessing at the appropriate time.

We keep from getting discouraged by keeping our eyes on the goal and our future rewards with God in heaven.

PROMISE FROM GOD:

Matthew 10:22
Everyone will hate you because of your allegiance to me. But those who endure to the end will be saved.

○○○ Racism ○○○

What does the Bible say about racism?

John 4:9
She said to Jesus, "You are a Jew, and I am a Samaritan woman. Why are you asking me for a drink?"

○○○ Although Samaritans were seen as half-breeds and were hated by the Jews of his day, Jesus went out of his way to have a life-changing conversation with one sinful Samaritan woman.

Luke 10:33
Then a despised Samaritan came along.

○○○ Jesus confused his listeners by making a hated Samaritan the hero of one of his most famous stories.

Colossians 3:11
In this new life, it doesn't matter if you are a Jew or a Gentile.

○○○ Our churches should welcome all races.

Ephesians 2:14
Christ himself has made peace between us Jews and you Gentiles by making us all one people. He has broken down the wall of hostility that used to separate us.

○○○ Christ died to destroy all the barriers of hatred that sin had created between people. We must not rebuild those walls.

PROMISE FROM GOD:

Galatians 3:28
There is no longer Jew or Gentile. . . . For you are all Christians—you are one in Christ Jesus.

○○○ Rebellion ○○○

What does it mean to rebel against God?

Numbers 20:12
You did not trust me enough to demonstrate my holiness to the people of Israel.

○○○ Moses rebelled when he did not trust God and disobeyed God's instructions.

Jeremiah 1:16
They worship idols that they themselves have made!

Matthew 6:21
Wherever your treasure is, there your heart and thoughts will also be.

○○○ We rebel against God whenever we love other things more than him.

Judges 2:11-12
The Israelites . . . abandoned the Lord. . . . They chased after other gods, worshiping the gods of the people around them.

○○○ When our rebellion leads to idolatry, we are in danger of destruction.

Isaiah 59:2
Your sins have cut you off from God.

1 John 3:4
Those who sin are opposed to the law of God.

○○○ Sin is rebellion against God, wanting to do things our own way. When we rebel against God, we become separated from him.

1 Samuel 12:15
If you rebel against the Lord's commands and refuse to listen to him, then his hand will be as heavy upon you as it was upon your ancestors.

••• Rebellion is refusing to listen to and obey God.

Ezekiel 20:13
They wouldn't obey my instructions even though obedience would have given them life.

••• Sometimes our rebellion can be so stubborn that we refuse to obey even when obedience would help us.

Hebrews 3:12
Be careful then, dear brothers and sisters. Make sure that your own hearts are not evil and unbelieving, turning you away from the living God.

••• The ultimate spiritual rebellion is refusing to accept God's offer of salvation through Jesus Christ.

Hosea 11:11
"I will bring them home again," says the Lord.

••• No matter how far a rebel strays, God still loves that person.

Is rebellion ever good?

1 Peter 4:3
You have had enough in the past of the evil things that godless people enjoy.

••• When you're pressured to take part in something wrong, you must rebel against those who are pressuring you.

Matthew 21:12
Jesus entered the Temple and began to drive out the merchants.

••• Jesus himself rebelled against sin and corruption in his temple.

PROMISE FROM GOD:

Jeremiah 3:22
"My wayward children," says the Lord, "come back to me, and I will heal your wayward hearts."

••• Reconciliation •••

What is reconciliation, and how can we be reconciled to God?

Isaiah 53:5
He was wounded and crushed for our sins. He was beaten that we might have peace. He was whipped, and we were healed!

Romans 5:10
Since we were restored to friendship with God by the death of his Son while we were still his enemies, we will certainly be delivered from eternal punishment by his life.

Ephesians 2:13
Now you belong to Christ Jesus. Though you once were far away from God, now you have been brought near to him because of the blood of Christ.

Colossians 1:20-21
By him God reconciled everything to himself. He made peace with everything in heaven and on earth by means of his blood on the cross. This includes you who were once so far away from God.

ooo Being reconciled means finding peace with each other again, being reunited. Through Jesus' death for our sins, God has made it possible for us to be reconciled to him.

Romans 5:1
Since we have been made right in God's sight by faith, we have peace with God because of what Jesus Christ our Lord has done for us.

2 Corinthians 5:19-21
God was in Christ, reconciling the world to himself, no longer counting people's sins against them. This is the wonderful message he has given us to tell others. We are Christ's ambassadors, and God is using us to speak to you. We urge you, as though Christ himself were here pleading with you, "Be reconciled to God!" For God made Christ, who never sinned, to be the offering for our sin, so that we could be made right with God through Christ.

Colossians 2:14
He canceled the record that contained the charges against us. He took it and destroyed it by nailing it to Christ's cross.

ooo In order to be reconciled with God, we must believe in what Jesus Christ has done for us.

Why is reconciliation between people important?

Matthew 5:23-24
If you are standing before the altar in the Temple, offering a sacrifice to God, and you suddenly remember that someone has something against you, leave your sacrifice there beside the altar. Go and be reconciled to that person. Then come and offer your sacrifice to God.

∘∘∘ Being reconciled to other people is important to our relationship with God.

Matthew 5:25-26
Come to terms quickly with your enemy before it is too late and you are dragged into court, handed over to an officer, and thrown in jail. I assure you that you won't be free again until you have paid the last penny.

∘∘∘ Working for reconciliation with others is wise.

Matthew 18:15
If another believer sins against you, go privately and point out the fault. If the other person listens and confesses it, you have won that person back.

∘∘∘ God wants us to resolve our differences with others because doing so brings unity.

How can people involved in conflict solve their differences?

Genesis 33:8-11
"What were all the flocks and herds I met as I came?" Esau asked. Jacob replied, "They are gifts, my lord, to ensure your goodwill." "Brother, I have plenty," Esau answered. "Keep what you have." "No, please accept them," Jacob said, "for what a relief it is to see your friendly smile. It is like seeing the smile of God! Please take my gifts, for God has been very generous to me. I have more than enough." Jacob continued to insist, so Esau finally accepted them.

∘∘∘ Giving gifts can be an important part of being reconciled to other people.

Ephesians 2:14
Christ himself has made peace between us Jews and you Gentiles by making us all one people. He has broken down the wall of hostility that used to separate us.

Through Christ, God has made a way for groups to make peace with each other and be fully reconciled.

Ephesians 1:10
This is his plan: At the right time he will bring everything together under the authority of Christ—everything in heaven and on earth.

In Christ's kingdom there will be peace between all people.

PROMISE FROM GOD:

Colossians 1:21-22
You were his enemies, separated from him by your evil thoughts and actions, yet now he has brought you back as his friends. He has done this through his death on the cross in his own human body. As a result, he has brought you into the very presence of God, and you are holy and blameless as you stand before him without a single fault.

Reliability

See Responsibility

◦◦◦ Repentance ◦◦◦

Why does God want us to repent?

Leviticus 26:40
But at last my people will confess their sins and the sins of their ancestors for betraying me and being hostile toward me.

◦◦◦ All of us need to repent because we have hurt God with our sins.

2 Chronicles 30:9
The Lord your God is gracious and merciful. If you return to him, he will not continue to turn his face from you.

◦◦◦ Repentance is necessary to keep a good relationship with God.

Proverbs 28:13
People who cover over their sins will not prosper. But if they confess and forsake them, they will receive mercy.

Isaiah 55:7
Let the people turn from their wicked deeds. Let them banish from their minds the very thought of doing wrong! Let them turn to the Lord that he may have mercy on them. Yes, turn to our God, for he will abundantly pardon.

Jeremiah 3:12
Therefore, go and say these words to Israel, "This is what the Lord says: O Israel, my faithless people, come home to me again, for I am merciful. I will not be angry with you forever."

◦◦◦ Repentance is necessary to receive God's mercy.

Ezekiel 18:30-32
I will judge each of you, O people of Israel, according to your actions, says the Sovereign Lord. Turn from your sins! Don't let

them destroy you! Put all your rebellion behind you, and get for yourselves a new heart and a new spirit. For why should you die, O people of Israel? I don't want you to die, says the Sovereign Lord. Turn back and live!

Ezekiel 33:11
As surely as I live, says the Sovereign Lord, I take no pleasure in the death of wicked people. I only want them to turn from their wicked ways so they can live. Turn! Turn from your wickedness, O people of Israel! Why should you die?

••• Repentance is the key to having new life from God.

Matthew 3:2
Turn from your sins and turn to God, because the Kingdom of Heaven is near.

Luke 24:47
There is forgiveness of sins for all who turn to me.

Acts 2:37-38
Peter's words convicted them deeply, and they said to him and to the other apostles, "Brothers, what should we do?" Peter replied, "Each of you must turn from your sins and turn to God, and be baptized in the name of Jesus Christ for the forgiveness of your sins. Then you will receive the gift of the Holy Spirit."

••• Forgiveness of sins and entrance to the kingdom of heaven is only for those who have turned away from their sins and turned to God.

Matthew 11:20, 23
Jesus began to denounce the cities where he had done most of his miracles, because they hadn't turned from their sins and turned to God. . . . "You people of Capernaum, will you be exalted to heaven? No, you will be brought down to the place of the dead."

Refusal to turn away from our sins will bring God's judgment.

PROMISE FROM GOD:

2 Chronicles 7:14
If my people who are called by my name will humble themselves and pray and seek my face and turn from their wicked ways, I will hear from heaven and will forgive their sins and heal their land.

Reputation

Should Christians be concerned about their reputation?

2 Corinthians 8:20
We are anxious that no one should find fault with the way we are handling this generous gift.

We must work hard to build a good reputation so that our actions don't keep people from accepting Christ's Good News of salvation.

Matthew 6:1
Don't do your good deeds publicly, to be admired.

Jesus warns us not to do good things in order to impress others.

2 Peter 1:5
Your faith will produce a life of moral excellence.

Our belief in Jesus should show in our life.

How can a bad reputation be changed?

1 Peter 2:12
They will see your honorable behavior, and they will believe and give honor to God.

••• The best way to have a good reputation is to have good behavior.

Deuteronomy 4:6
If you obey [God's laws] carefully, you will display your wisdom and intelligence to the surrounding nations.

••• Obedience to God brings a reputation for being smart and wise.

Mark 2:16
They said to his disciples, "Why does [Jesus] eat with such scum?"

••• We don't have to have a good reputation in order for Jesus to accept us. He accepts us because of his love, which can change sinners.

3 John 1:3
Some of the brothers recently returned and made me very happy by telling me about your faithfulness and that you are living in the truth.

••• Christians should earn the reputation of obeying God's standards for purity and truth.

PROMISE FROM GOD:

1 Peter 5:6
Humble yourselves under the mighty power of God, and in his good time he will honor you.

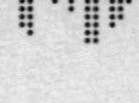

◦◦◦ Responsibility ◦◦◦

How can I develop responsibility?

Matthew 25:20-21, 24-26
The servant to whom he had entrusted the five bags of gold said, "Sir, you gave me five bags of gold to invest, and I have doubled the amount." The master was full of praise. "Well done, my good and faithful servant. You have been faithful in handling this small amount, so now I will give you many more responsibilities. Let's celebrate together!" . . . Then the servant with the one bag of gold came and said, "Sir, I know you are a hard man, harvesting crops you didn't plant and gathering crops you didn't cultivate. I was afraid I would lose your money, so I hid it in the earth and here it is." But the master replied, "You wicked and lazy servant! You think I'm a hard man, do you, harvesting crops I didn't plant and gathering crops I didn't cultivate?"

Galatians 6:5
We are each responsible for our own conduct.

◦◦◦ We develop responsibility by conscientiously obeying God's Word and doing what is right.

Romans 12:3
As God's messenger, I give each of you this warning: Be honest in your estimate of yourselves, measuring your value by how much faith God has given you.

◦◦◦ You can become more responsible by figuring out how much responsibility you can handle and then making sure that you handle it well.

Proverbs 3:11-12
My child, don't ignore it when the Lord disciplines you, and

don't be discouraged when he corrects you. For the Lord corrects those he loves, just as a father corrects a child in whom he delights.

Hebrews 12:11
No discipline is enjoyable while it is happening—it is painful! But afterward there will be a quiet harvest of right living for those who are trained in this way.

God will train you to be more responsible if you let him work in your heart and life.

Should I be held responsible for things that are not my fault?

Genesis 3:12-13
"Yes," Adam admitted, "but it was the woman you gave me who brought me the fruit, and I ate it." Then the Lord God asked the woman, "How could you do such a thing?" "The serpent tricked me," she replied. "That's why I ate it."

Genesis 16:5
Sarai said to Abram, "It's all your fault! Now this servant of mine is pregnant, and she despises me, though I myself gave her the privilege of sleeping with you. The Lord will make you pay for doing this to me!"

Exodus 32:22-24
"Don't get upset, sir," Aaron replied. "You yourself know these people and what a wicked bunch they are. They said to me, 'Make us some gods to lead us, for something has happened to this man Moses, who led us out of Egypt.' So I told them, 'Bring me your gold earrings.' When they brought them to me, I threw them into the fire—and out came this calf!"

Matthew 27:24
Pilate saw that he wasn't getting anywhere and that a riot was

developing. So he sent for a bowl of water and washed his hands before the crowd, saying, "I am innocent of the blood of this man. The responsibility is yours!"

●●● Sometimes we try to pass the buck for things that we really *are* responsible for.

1 Chronicles 21:7-8, 17
God was very displeased with the census, and he punished Israel for it. Then David said to God, "I have sinned greatly and shouldn't have taken the census. Please forgive me for doing this foolish thing." And David said to God, "I am the one who called for the census! I am the one who has sinned and done wrong! But these people are innocent—what have they done? O Lord my God, let your anger fall against me and my family, but do not destroy your people."

●●● Sometimes it does seem that God is punishing innocent people for the sins of others. We should realize instead that innocent people sometimes suffer because of others' sins.

Numbers 14:20-23
The Lord said, ". . . As surely as I live, and as surely as the earth is filled with the Lord's glory, not one of these people will ever enter that land. They have seen my glorious presence and the miraculous signs I performed both in Egypt and in the wilderness, but again and again they tested me by refusing to listen. They will never even see the land I swore to give their ancestors. None of those who have treated me with contempt will enter it."

Numbers 14:24
My servant Caleb is different from the others. He has remained loyal to me, and I will bring him into the land he explored. His descendants will receive their full share of that land.

Those who are clearly innocent should not be punished with the guilty.

Deuteronomy 24:16
Parents must not be put to death for the sins of their children, nor the children for the sins of their parents. Those worthy of death must be executed for their own crimes.

Ezekiel 18:1-4
Another message came to me from the Lord: "Why do you quote this proverb in the land of Israel: 'The parents have eaten sour grapes, but their children's mouths pucker at the taste'? As surely as I live, says the Sovereign Lord, you will not say this proverb anymore in Israel. For all people are mine to judge—both parents and children alike. And this is my rule: The person who sins will be the one who dies."

In terms of judgment before God, a person is held responsible only for his or her own sins. God will not judge or punish you for someone else's sins. But unfortunately, sin's consequences affect others. Sin almost always hurts others and not just the sinner.

PROMISE FROM GOD:

Matthew 25:29
To those who use well what they are given, even more will be given, and they will have an abundance. But from those who are unfaithful, even what little they have will be taken away.

● ● ● Resurrection ● ● ●

How can I have confidence that God will someday resurrect me to heaven?

1 Corinthians 15:12-14
Tell me this—since we preach that Christ rose from the dead, why are some of you saying there will be no resurrection of the dead? For if there is no resurrection of the dead, then Christ has not been raised either. And if Christ was not raised, then all our preaching is useless, and your trust in God is useless.

● ● ● If Christ had not defeated death, there would be no hope for you or me. The fact that Christ *did* come back to life proves that God will keep his promise to raise us from the dead.

What does Jesus' resurrection mean to me?

John 3:16
God so loved the world that he gave his only Son, so that everyone who believes in him will not perish but have eternal life.

1 Corinthians 15:42
It is the same way for the resurrection of the dead. Our earthly bodies, which die and decay, will be different when they are resurrected, for they will never die.

● ● ● Jesus' resurrection was God's plan to allow us to spend eternity with him. Because Jesus was raised from the dead, we can be sure that he has power over death and that Christians, too, will be resurrected one day and will live forever with him in heaven.

What will my body be like after it is resurrected?

1 Corinthians 15:43-44
Our bodies now disappoint us, but when they are raised, they will be full of glory. They are weak now, but when they are raised, they will be full of power. They are natural human bodies now, but when they are raised, they will be spiritual bodies. For just as there are natural bodies, so also there are spiritual bodies.

If you are disappointed with your body now, you won't be when you get to heaven. Our resurrected bodies will be full of power, strength, and freshness.

PROMISE FROM GOD:

John 11:25-26
Jesus told her, "I am the resurrection and the life. Those who believe in me, even though they die like everyone else, will live again. They are given eternal life for believing in me and will never perish."

Ridicule

How does God want me to deal with ridicule?

2 Chronicles 30:10
The messengers went from town to town throughout Ephraim and Manasseh and as far as the territory of Zebulun. But most of the people just laughed at the messengers and made fun of them.

Ridicule is nothing more than mean words aimed to hurt another person.

Nehemiah 4:4
I prayed, "Hear us, O our God, for we are being mocked. May their scoffing fall back on their own heads."

Nehemiah handled ridicule with prayer.

Matthew 5:11-12
God blesses you when you are mocked and persecuted and lied about because you are my followers. Be happy about it! Be very glad! For a great reward awaits you in heaven. And remember, the ancient prophets were persecuted, too.

Know that those who are faithful to God even through persecution and ridicule will receive a great reward in heaven.

PROMISE FROM GOD:

1 Peter 4:14
Be happy if you are insulted for being a Christian, for then the glorious Spirit of God will come upon you.

Right and Wrong

How can I tell what is really right or wrong, no matter what other people say?

Exodus 20:1
Then God instructed the people.

John 14:15
If you love me, obey my commandments.

John 14:17
He is the Holy Spirit, who leads into all truth.

Proverbs 21:2
People may think they are doing what is right, but the Lord examines the heart.

Romans 8:5
Those who are dominated by the sinful nature think about sinful things, but those who are controlled by the Holy Spirit think about things that please the Spirit.

Galatians 5:16
So I advise you to live according to your new life in the Holy Spirit. Then you won't be doing what your sinful nature craves.

God has given us the Holy Spirit, who will help us live obediently. He will alert us when our old sinful nature is trying to take over. God has also given us his Word, the Bible, which clearly tells us absolute right and wrong.

Some friends make fun of me for doing right. How do I deal with that?

1 Peter 3:14
Even if you suffer for doing what is right, God will reward you for it. So don't be afraid and don't worry.

Genesis 18:19
Keep the way of the Lord and do what is right and just. Then I will do . . . all that I have promised.

Romans 2:10
There will be glory and honor and peace from God for all who do good.

Have you ever wondered why you feel good after doing something you know is right? God promises us peace when we do what is right.

PROMISE FROM GOD:

2 Timothy 3:16
All Scripture is inspired by God and is useful to teach us what is true and to make us realize what is wrong in our lives. It straightens us out and teaches us to do what is right.

Salvation

What does it mean to be saved?

Romans 4:8
What joy for those whose sin is no longer counted against them by the Lord.

Romans 3:24
God in his gracious kindness declares us not guilty.

Being saved means no longer having our sins count against us. It means being forgiven by the mercy of God.

Psalm 103:12
He has removed our rebellious acts as far away from us as the east is from the west.

Being saved means that our sins have been completely removed.

Psalm 51:9-10
Remove the stain of my guilt. Create in me a clean heart, O God.

Being saved means that our guilt has been washed away.

1 Peter 2:10
Once you received none of God's mercy; now you have received his mercy.

Romans 3:24
He has done this through Christ Jesus, who has freed us by taking away our sins.

ooo Being saved means that we are forgiven in Christ.

How can I be saved?

Romans 10:13
Anyone who calls on the name of the Lord will be saved.

ooo God's Word promises salvation to anyone who calls on Jesus' name.

John 3:16
God so loved the world that he gave his only Son, so that everyone who believes in him will not perish but have eternal life.

John 5:24
I assure you, those who listen to my message and believe in God who sent me have eternal life.

ooo Jesus himself promised that those who believe in him will be saved.

Is salvation available to anyone?

John 3:16
God so loved the world that he gave his only Son, so that everyone who believes in him will not perish but have eternal life.

ooo Anyone can receive salvation by believing in Jesus Christ and his message of the Good News.

Hebrews 9:27
It is destined that each person dies only once and after that comes judgment.

ooo Salvation is available to all, but a time will come when it will be too late to receive it.

How can I be sure of my salvation?

John 1:12
To all who believed him and accepted him, he gave the right to become children of God.

ooo Just as a child cannot be "un-born," God's children—those who have believed in Jesus Christ—cannot be "un-born-again."

Romans 8:14
All who are led by the Spirit of God are children of God.

ooo The Holy Spirit lives in our heart and helps us know that we are God's children.

Matthew 14:30-31
"Save me, Lord!" he shouted. Instantly Jesus reached out his hand and grabbed him.

ooo We cannot save ourselves from sin, guilt, judgment, and spiritual death. Only Jesus Christ can save us.

Why is salvation such a big part of Christianity?

Genesis 6:11, 13
The earth had become corrupt in God's sight. . . . So God said to Noah, "I have decided to destroy all living creatures."

Romans 6:23
The wages of sin is death.

ooo Salvation is necessary because our sin separates us from the holy God. Our sin brings judgment and spiritual death.

Exodus 12:23
When he sees the blood on the top and sides of the doorframe, the Lord will pass over your home. He will not permit the Destroyer to enter and strike down your firstborn.

Salvation through Jesus was written about long before he was born. God let people know ahead of time that he had a plan to save them from sin.

Acts 4:12
There is salvation in no one else! There is no other name in all of heaven for people to call on to save them.

Because we are sinful, we need to be rescued—"saved"—from destruction. Jesus Christ provides this salvation when we ask him to save us.

PROMISE FROM GOD:

Romans 10:9
If you confess with your mouth that Jesus is Lord and believe in your heart that God raised him from the dead, you will be saved.

Self-Control

Why can't I seem to control certain desires?

Galatians 5:24
Those who belong to Christ Jesus have nailed the passions and desires of their sinful nature to his cross.

One reason for a lack of self-control may be that you haven't yet become God's child through accepting Jesus Christ as your Savior. If that's true about you, it's important to put your faith in him right away.

Romans 12:1
And so, dear brothers and sisters, I plead with you to give your bodies to God. Let them be a living and holy sacrifice—the kind he will accept.

The way to become pure is to give ourselves completely to God. If we try to hang on to just a little sin, it will eventually rule us.

What are some ways to practice self-control?

Psalm 119:9
How can a young person stay pure? By obeying your word and following its rules.

2 Timothy 2:5
Follow the Lord's rules for doing his work, just as an athlete either follows the rules or is disqualified and wins no prize.

To have self-control you must first know what God's Word says about right living. You need to know what you must control before you can keep it under control. Reading God's Word every day keeps his guidelines in mind.

Psalm 141:3
Take control of what I say, O Lord, and keep my lips sealed.

Proverbs 10:19
Don't talk too much. . . . Be sensible and turn off the flow!

Proverbs 13:3
Those who control their tongue will have a long life; a quick retort can ruin everything.

Matthew 12:36
I tell you this, that you must give an account on judgment day of every idle word you speak.

Ephesians 4:29
Don't use foul or abusive language. Let everything you say be good and helpful, so that your words will be an encouragement to those who hear them.

James 1:26
If you claim to be religious but don't control your tongue, you are just fooling yourself, and your religion is worthless.

We show self-control by watching what we say. We often wish we could take back words as soon as they've left our mouth!

Romans 13:14
Let the Lord Jesus Christ take control of you, and don't think of ways to indulge your evil desires.

2 Peter 1:6
Knowing God leads to self-control. Self-control leads to patient endurance, and patient endurance leads to godliness.

We need to ask God to help us with self-control. The better we know God, the easier self-control becomes.

When we need help beyond our own self-control, what should we do?

Psalm 56:3-4
When I am afraid, I put my trust in you. O God, I praise your word. I trust in God, so why should I be afraid? What can mere mortals do to me?

Psalm 60:12
With God's help we will do mighty things, for he will trample down our foes.

Psalm 61:2
From the ends of the earth, I will cry to you for help, for my heart is overwhelmed. Lead me to the towering rock of safety.

God works through our weakness. When we face a problem or temptation, we should run to God for help.

Sometimes I feel as if I'm the only one who faces temptations.

1 Corinthians 10:13
Remember that the temptations that come into your life are no different from what others experience. . . . When you are tempted, [God] will show you a way out so that you will not give in to it.

It helps to know that others face the same temptations we do. It also helps to know that God wants to help us! Ask him.

What are the rewards of self-control?

James 1:12
God blesses the people who patiently endure testing. Afterward they will receive the crown of life that God has promised to those who love him.

God will reward in heaven those who practice self-control on earth.

PROMISE FROM GOD:

2 Peter 1:6
Knowing God leads to self-control. Self-control leads to patient endurance, and patient endurance leads to godliness.

○○○ Sin ○○○

What are the consequences of sin?

Exodus 34:7
I show this unfailing love to many thousands by forgiving every kind of sin and rebellion. Even so I do not leave sin unpunished.

Leviticus 5:17
If any of them sin by doing something forbidden by the Lord, even if it is done unintentionally, they will be held responsible.

Proverbs 11:21
You can be sure that evil people will be punished.

Ecclesiastes 12:14
God will judge us for everything we do, including every secret thing, whether good or bad.

Isaiah 13:11
I, the Lord, will punish the world for its evil and the wicked for their sin.

Ezekiel 18:4
The person who sins will be the one who dies.

Malachi 4:1
The Lord Almighty says, "The day of judgment is coming, burning like a furnace. The arrogant and the wicked will be burned up like straw on that day. They will be consumed like a tree—roots and all."

○○○ Sin brings God's punishment because it breaks God's laws and offends his holiness.

Numbers 32:23
You may be sure that your sin will find you out.

Proverbs 5:22
An evil man is held captive by his own sins; they are ropes that catch and hold him.

●●● Our sins come back on us. Eventually we'll face consequences.

Isaiah 59:2
There is a problem—your sins have cut you off from God. Because of your sin, he has turned away and will not listen anymore.

●●● Sin has separated us from God.

Luke 23:41
We deserve to die for our evil deeds.

Romans 2:9
There will be trouble and calamity for everyone who keeps on sinning—for the Jew first and also for the Gentile.

Romans 6:23
The wages of sin is death.

Ephesians 2:1
Once you were dead, doomed forever because of your many sins.

2 Thessalonians 1:9
They will be punished with everlasting destruction, forever separated from the Lord and from his glorious power.

Revelation 20:15
Anyone whose name was not found recorded in the Book of Life was thrown into the lake of fire.

●●● The penalty for our sins is death—physical death and eternal judgment by God.

Is there a way to be free from sin?

Psalm 19:12
How can I know all the sins lurking in my heart? Cleanse me from these hidden faults.

Psalm 51:2-3
Wash me clean from my guilt. Purify me from my sin. For I recognize my shameful deeds—they haunt me day and night.

Psalm 139:23-24
Search me, O God, and know my heart; test me and know my thoughts. Point out anything in me that offends you, and lead me along the path of everlasting life.

Ask God to cleanse your heart from sin.

Isaiah 1:18
"Come now, let us argue this out," says the Lord. "No matter how deep the stain of your sins, I can remove it. I can make you as clean as freshly fallen snow. Even if you are stained as red as crimson, I can make you as white as wool."

Zechariah 13:1
On that day a fountain will be opened for the dynasty of David and for the people of Jerusalem, a fountain to cleanse them from all their sins and defilement.

Matthew 26:28
This is my blood, which seals the covenant between God and his people. It is poured out to forgive the sins of many.

2 Corinthians 5:21
God made Christ, who never sinned, to be the offering for our sin, so that we could be made right with God through Christ.

Hebrews 9:14
Just think how much more the blood of Christ will purify our

hearts from deeds that lead to death so that we can worship the living God.

◡◡◡ God has made it possible for our sin to be removed through Jesus' death in our place.

Ezra 10:11
Confess your sin to the Lord, the God of your ancestors, and do what he demands.

Isaiah 1:16
Wash yourselves and be clean! Let me no longer see your evil deeds. Give up your wicked ways.

1 John 1:9
If we confess our sins to him, he is faithful and just to forgive us and to cleanse us from every wrong.

◡◡◡ When we confess our sins to God, he forgives us and forgets our sins.

Romans 6:6, 18
Our old sinful selves were crucified with Christ so that sin might lose its power in our lives. We are no longer slaves to sin. . . . Now you are free from sin, your old master, and you have become slaves to your new master, righteousness.

Galatians 5:24
Those who belong to Christ Jesus have nailed the passions and desires of their sinful nature to his cross and crucified them there.

◡◡◡ Because of what Christ has done, those who have faith in God are free from the power of sin.

PROMISES FROM GOD:

1 Peter 2:24
He personally carried away our sins in his own body on the cross so we can be dead to sin and live for what is right. You have been healed by his wounds!

2 Peter 2:9
The Lord knows how to rescue godly people from their trials, even while punishing the wicked right up until the day of judgment.

Strengths and Weaknesses

How can I know what my strengths and weaknesses are?

Ephesians 1:16-17
I have never stopped thanking God for you. I pray for you constantly, asking God, the glorious Father of our Lord Jesus Christ, to give you spiritual wisdom and understanding, so that you might grow in your knowledge of God.

The more you know God, the better you will understand your own strengths and weaknesses.

Daniel 1:4
"Select only strong, healthy, and good-looking young men," [the king] said. "Make sure they are well versed in every branch of learning, are gifted with knowledge and good sense, and have the poise needed to serve in the royal palace. Teach these young men the language and literature of the Babylonians."

Matthew 25:15
He gave five bags of gold to one, two bags of gold to another, and one bag of gold to the last—dividing it in proportion to their abilities—and then left on his trip.

1 Timothy 4:14
Do not neglect the spiritual gift you received through the prophecies spoken to you when the elders of the church laid their hands on you.

Others around us will notice what our strengths are.

Exodus 31:3
I have filled him with the Spirit of God, giving him great wisdom, intelligence, and skill in all kinds of crafts.

Romans 12:6
God has given each of us the ability to do certain things well. So if God has given you the ability to prophesy, speak out when you have faith that God is speaking through you.

God has given each of us gifts to use for him.

PROMISES FROM GOD:

Isaiah 40:29-31
He gives power to those who are tired and worn out; he offers strength to the weak. Even youths will become exhausted, and young men will give up. But those who wait on the Lord will find new strength. They will fly high on wings like eagles. They will run and not grow weary. They will walk and not faint.

Isaiah 41:10
Don't be afraid, for I am with you. Do not be dismayed, for I am your God. I will strengthen you. I will help you. I will uphold you with my victorious right hand.

◦◦◦ Success ◦◦◦

What is true success?

Acts 16:31
Believe on the Lord Jesus and you will be saved.

◦◦◦ Having faith in Jesus is true success.

Matthew 22:37
Jesus replied, "You must love the Lord your God with all your heart, all your soul, and all your mind."

◦◦◦ True success involves wholehearted love for God.

1 Kings 2:3
Observe the requirements of the Lord your God and follow all his ways.

Psalm 119:115
I intend to obey the commands of my God.

◦◦◦ Obedience to God's Word brings true success.

Matthew 20:26
Among you it should be quite different. Whoever wants to be a leader among you must be your servant.

◦◦◦ Serving and helping others makes us successful in God's eyes.

Proverbs 16:3
Commit your work to the Lord, and then your plans will succeed.

◦◦◦ Committing all we do to God and putting him first in our life brings success on God's terms.

Mark 4:19
All too quickly the message is crowded out by the cares of this life, the lure of wealth, and the desire for nice things.

••• True success, which comes from God, is impossible if we run after worldly things that pull us away from him.

Is it okay to try to be successful?

Proverbs 12:24
Work hard and become a leader; be lazy and become a slave.

Proverbs 22:29
Do you see any truly competent workers? They will serve kings rather than ordinary people.

••• There are many godly character traits that we should have. Traits such as hard work, integrity, commitment, serving others, and wisdom often bring success.

Genesis 39:2-3
The Lord was with Joseph and blessed him greatly as he served in the home of his Egyptian master . . . giving him success in everything he did.

Exodus 33:14
The Lord replied, "I will personally go with you . . . everything will be fine for you."

••• The Scriptures have frequent references to God's blessings for his people. God allows his people to have material blessing but urges them never to sacrifice spiritual riches for worldly wealth.

What is the right perspective on accomplishments?

Ecclesiastes 12:13
Here is my final conclusion: Fear God and obey his commands, for this is the duty of every person.

••• Obeying God is life's greatest accomplishment.

Is accomplishment just the fruit of hard work, or is there something else to it?

Romans 1:17
This Good News tells us how God makes us right in his sight. This is accomplished from start to finish by faith. As the Scriptures say, "It is through faith that a righteous person has life."

••• We prepare for heaven and eternity with God by believing that Jesus Christ died for our sins so that we wouldn't have to. Salvation, the greatest accomplishment, is not the work of our hands but the work of God in our heart.

How do we make the most of our accomplishments?

Ecclesiastes 4:9
Two people can accomplish more than twice as much as one; they get a better return for their labor.

••• It is impossible for one person to play a duet or a trio. It is hard to play football or soccer without teamwork. Two people can actually do more than twice as much as one—as long as they are pulling in the same direction.

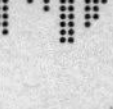

Is it wrong to be proud of our accomplishments?

1 Corinthians 4:7
What makes you better than anyone else? What do you have that God hasn't given you? And if all you have is from God, why boast as though you have accomplished something on your own?

●●● It's okay to be happy with the good feeling of accomplishment, as long as we thank God for giving us his power. But it is wrong to think we did it all by ourselves.

PROMISE FROM GOD:

Psalm 60:12
With God's help we will do mighty things.

●●● *Suffering* ●●●

Why am I suffering? Doesn't God care about me?

Genesis 37:28
When the traders came by, his brothers pulled Joseph out of the pit and sold him for twenty pieces of silver.

Jeremiah 32:18
You are loving and kind to thousands, though children suffer for their parents' sins.

●●● Sometimes we suffer because of the sins of others and not because of our own sins.

John 9:2-3
"Teacher," his disciples asked him, "why was this man born blind? Was it a result of his own sins or those of his parents?" "It was not because of his sins or his parents' sins," Jesus answered.

●●● Sometimes the suffering that comes to us is not our fault. The way we react to the suffering is the key.

Genesis 3:6, 23
The fruit looked so fresh and delicious. . . . So she ate some of the fruit. . . . The Lord God banished Adam and his wife from the Garden of Eden.

Leviticus 26:43
At last the people will receive the due punishment for their sins, for they rejected my regulations and despised my laws.

Proverbs 3:11-12
My child, don't ignore it when the Lord disciplines you. . . . For the Lord corrects those he loves, just as a father corrects a child in whom he delights.

●●● Sometimes God sends suffering as a consequence of our sins. He disciplines us because he loves us and wants to correct us and restore us to himself.

Deuteronomy 8:2
Remember how the Lord your God led you through the wilderness for forty years, humbling you and testing you . . . to find out whether or not you would really obey his commands.

●●● Sometimes God tests us with suffering to encourage us to obey him.

1 Peter 4:14
Be happy if you are insulted for being a Christian, for then the glorious Spirit of God will come upon you.

••• Sometimes we suffer because we must take a stand for Christ.

James 1:3
When your faith is tested, your endurance has a chance to grow.

••• Sometimes we willingly suffer because it will help us grow and mature.

2 Timothy 3:12
Yes, and everyone who wants to live a godly life in Christ Jesus will suffer persecution.

••• The world hates Christ, so when we identify with him, we can expect the world that inflicted suffering on him to also inflict suffering on us.

Can any good come from suffering?

Job 5:17-18
Consider the joy of those corrected by God! Do not despise the chastening of the Almighty when you sin. For though he wounds, he also bandages. He strikes, but his hands also heal.

••• Suffering can bring great renewal and healing.

Romans 5:3-4
We can rejoice, too, when we run into problems and trials, for we know that they are good for us—they help us learn to endure. And endurance develops strength of character.

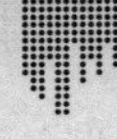

2 Corinthians 1:5
You can be sure that the more we suffer for Christ, the more God will shower us with his comfort through Christ.

2 Corinthians 12:10
Since I know it is all for Christ's good, I am quite content with my weaknesses and with insults, hardships, persecutions, and calamities. For when I am weak, then I am strong.

2 Timothy 2:10
I am willing to endure anything if it will bring salvation and eternal glory in Christ Jesus to those God has chosen.

Hebrews 12:11
No discipline is enjoyable while it is happening—it is painful! But afterward there will be a quiet harvest of right living for those who are trained in this way.

James 1:3-4
When your faith is tested, your endurance has a chance to grow. . . . For when your endurance is fully developed, you will be strong in character and ready for anything.

When something is for our good, Christ's glory, and the building of his church, we should be happy to accept it even though it involves suffering.

How can I stay close to God in times of suffering?

Psalm 22:24
He has not ignored the suffering of the needy. He has not turned and walked away. He has listened to their cries for help.

Recognize that God has not left us in times of suffering.

Psalm 126:5-6
Those who plant in tears will harvest with shouts of joy. They weep as they go to plant their seed, but they sing as they return with the harvest.

●●● Recognize that suffering is not forever. When we suffer it's hard to think of a future filled with joy and gladness. But God will change our tears of suffering into joy.

Lamentations 3:32-33
Though he brings grief, he also shows compassion according to the greatness of his unfailing love. For he does not enjoy hurting people or causing them sorrow.

●●● Recognize that God does not want to see us suffer. A loving God does not enjoy the hardships that must come our way to train us. But with his compassionate love and care, he sees us through our times of discipline and suffering.

Matthew 17:12
Soon the Son of Man will also suffer at their hands.

Luke 24:26
Wasn't it clearly predicted by the prophets that the Messiah would have to suffer all these things before entering his time of glory?

John 3:16
God so loved the world that he gave his only Son, so that everyone who believes in him will not perish but have eternal life.

●●● Recognize that Jesus himself suffered for us. Christ suffered a horrible death on the cross, which included both physical suffering and the spiritual agony of taking on the sins of the world.

Romans 8:17-18
Since we are his children, we will share his treasures—for everything God gives to his Son, Christ, is ours, too. But if we are to share his glory, we must also share his suffering. Yet what we suffer now is nothing compared to the glory he will give us later.

Hebrews 2:18
Since he himself has gone through suffering and temptation, he is able to help us when we are being tempted.

When we share the suffering of Christ, we also share his treasures.

PROMISE FROM GOD:

2 Corinthians 1:3-4
All praise to the God and Father of our Lord Jesus Christ. He is the source of every mercy and the God who comforts us. He comforts us in all our troubles so that we can comfort others. When others are troubled, we will be able to give them the same comfort God has given us.

Teamwork

See Cooperation

Temptation

Does temptation ever come from God?

James 1:13
God is never tempted to do wrong, and he never tempts anyone else either.

Mark 7:21-23
From within, out of a person's heart, come evil thoughts, sexual immorality, theft, murder, adultery, greed, wickedness, deceit, eagerness for lustful pleasure, envy, slander, pride, and foolishness. All these vile things come from within.

••• Temptation comes from inside a person's heart. Temptation never comes from God.

James 1:2
Whenever trouble comes your way, let it be an opportunity for joy.

••• Although God does not send temptation, he does delight in helping us grow stronger through it.

What makes temptation so hard to resist?

Genesis 3:6
The fruit looked so fresh and delicious. . . . So she ate some of the fruit.

••• Satan's favorite strategy is to make what is sinful appear to be desirable and good.

How can I avoid falling into temptation?

Genesis 39:12
[Joseph] ran from the house.

••• Often the best strategy against temptation is to flee the situation.

Proverbs 1:10
If sinners entice you, turn your back on them!

••• Avoid following the advice or actions of sinful people.

Matthew 6:13
Don't let us yield to temptation.

We should ask God to help us stand against temptation.

PROMISE FROM GOD:

1 Corinthians 10:13
Remember that the temptations that come into your life are no different from what others experience. And God is faithful. He will keep the temptation from becoming so strong that you can't stand up against it. When you are tempted, he will show you a way out so that you will not give in to it.

Truth

Who determines truth?

2 Samuel 7:28
You are God, O Sovereign Lord. Your words are truth.

Only God decides what is absolute truth.

Many say there is no such thing as absolute truth. How do we know the Bible is true?

Psalm 119:160
All your words are true; all your just laws will stand forever.

God's Word tells about God's truthful character.

John 16:13
When the Spirit of truth comes, he will guide you into all truth.

The Holy Spirit shows our mind and heart what is the truth.

John 18:37
Jesus said . . . "I came to bring truth to the world. All who love the truth recognize that what I say is true."

We find truth in Jesus Christ.

1 John 1:1
We saw him with our own eyes and touched him with our own hands.

We can trust that Christ's resurrection really happened because the story is told by eyewitnesses in the Bible.

Does God really expect us to tell the truth all the time?

Exodus 20:16
Do not testify falsely against your neighbor.

God's law clearly forbids lying.

Ephesians 4:15
We will hold to the truth in love.

God expects his followers to speak the truth always, in a loving way.

PROMISE FROM GOD:

Psalm 119:160
All your words are true; all your just laws will stand forever.

Values

How can I have godly values?

Genesis 39:8-9
Joseph refused. "Look," he told her, "my master trusts me with everything in his entire household. . . . How could I ever do such a wicked thing? It would be a great sin against God."

Refuse to give in to what is wrong.

Matthew 7:12
Do for others what you would like them to do for you. This is a summary of all that is taught in the law.

Galatians 5:22-23
When the Holy Spirit controls our lives, he will produce this kind of fruit in us: love, joy, peace, patience, kindness, goodness, faithfulness, gentleness, and self-control.

When God lives in us, we will have his values more and more.

Psalm 15:1-2
Who may worship in your sanctuary, Lord? . . . Those who lead blameless lives and do what is right, speaking the truth from sincere hearts.

Micah 6:8
The Lord has already told you what is good, and this is what he requires: to do what is right, to love mercy, and to walk humbly with your God.

Realize that God requires us to lead a godly life.

How can I figure out whether my current values are right?

Matthew 15:19
From the heart come evil thoughts, murder, adultery, all other sexual immorality, theft, lying, and slander.

Romans 1:29
Their lives became full of every kind of wickedness, sin, greed, hate, envy, murder, fighting, deception, malicious behavior, and gossip.

Ephesians 5:4
Obscene stories, foolish talk, and coarse jokes—these are not for you. Instead, let there be thankfulness to God.

Proverbs 30:8
Help me never to tell a lie.

Compare your values with the values found in the Bible.

How important is it for us to live consistent moral lives?

Psalm 24:3-4
Who may climb the mountain of the Lord? Who may stand in his holy place? Only those whose hands and hearts are pure.

Proverbs 28:2
When there is moral rot within a nation, its government topples easily.

Strong moral values are necessary to our own life with God and to the life of our society.

PROMISE FROM GOD:

Romans 5:3-5

We can rejoice, too, when we run into problems and trials, for we know that they are good for us—they help us learn to endure. And endurance develops strength of character in us, and character strengthens our confident expectation of salvation. And this expectation will not disappoint us. For we know how dearly God loves us, because he has given us the Holy Spirit to fill our hearts with his love.

Wisdom

How can we get wisdom?

Job 28:28

The fear of the Lord is true wisdom; to forsake evil is real understanding.

God gives wisdom to those who fear him and turn away from evil.

1 John 2:27

You have received the Holy Spirit, and he lives within you, so you don't need anyone to teach you what is true. For the Spirit teaches you all things, and what he teaches is true—it is not a lie. So continue in what he has taught you, and continue to live in Christ.

Wisdom comes from having a relationship with God.

Proverbs 1:5-6

Let those who are wise listen to these proverbs and become even wiser. And let those who understand receive guidance by exploring the depth of meaning in these proverbs, parables, wise sayings, and riddles.

ооо Obedience to God's Word—his commands, laws, and teachings—will make us wise.

Psalm 86:11
Teach me your ways, O Lord, that I may live according to your truth! Grant me purity of heart, that I may honor you.

James 1:5
If you need wisdom—if you want to know what God wants you to do—ask him, and he will gladly tell you. He will not resent your asking.

ооо If you need wisdom, ask God, and he will give it.

Colossians 3:16
Let the words of Christ, in all their richness, live in your hearts and make you wise. Use his words to teach and counsel each other.

ооо Listening to Christ's teachings and obeying his words will give you wisdom.

Proverbs 8:12, 17
I, Wisdom, live together with good judgment. I know where to discover knowledge and discernment. . . . I love all who love me. Those who search for me will surely find me.

ооо Those who seek wisdom are the ones who will find it.

PROMISE FROM GOD:

Proverbs 3:5-6
Trust in the Lord with all your heart; do not depend on your own understanding. Seek his will in all you do, and he will direct your paths.

◦◦◦ Witnessing ◦◦◦

How can I overcome my fear of witnessing?

Exodus 4:12
Now go, and do as I have told you. I will help you speak well, and I will tell you what to say.

Luke 21:15
I will give you the right words and such wisdom that none of your opponents will be able to reply!

◦◦◦ Trusting that God will speak through us will help us to overcome our fear of witnessing.

2 Corinthians 4:11, 13
Yes, we live under constant danger of death because we serve Jesus, so that the life of Jesus will be obvious in our dying bodies. . . . But we continue to preach because we have the same kind of faith the psalmist had when he said, "I believed in God, and so I speak."

◦◦◦ Even when we face death, faith in God can give us the courage to speak.

Psalm 27:1
The Lord is my light and my salvation—so why should I be afraid? The Lord protects me from danger—so why should I tremble?

Isaiah 44:8
Do not tremble; do not be afraid. Have I not proclaimed from ages past what my purposes are for you? You are my witnesses—is there any other God? No! There is no other Rock—not one!

Acts 18:9-10
One night the Lord spoke to Paul in a vision and told him, "Don't be afraid! Speak out! Don't be silent! For I am with you."

●●● Take courage and find strength in God's power, presence, and protection.

Ezekiel 2:6
Son of man, do not fear them. Don't be afraid even though their threats are sharp as thorns and barbed like briers, and they sting like scorpions. Do not be dismayed by their dark scowls. For remember, they are rebels!

●●● Be strong in God, and realize that rejection sometimes is just part of our job as witnesses for Christ.

Acts 4:18-20
So they called the apostles back in and told them never again to speak or teach about Jesus. But Peter and John replied, "Do you think God wants us to obey you rather than him? We cannot stop telling about the wonderful things we have seen and heard."

Acts 5:40
The council accepted his advice. They called in the apostles and had them flogged. Then they ordered them never again to speak in the name of Jesus, and they let them go.

●●● Realize that when you witness you are following in the footsteps of Christ and the apostles.

Acts 1:8
When the Holy Spirit has come upon you, you will receive power and will tell people about me everywhere—in Jerusalem, throughout Judea, in Samaria, and to the ends of the earth.

●●● The Holy Spirit will empower us and help us to speak.

1 Corinthians 2:4
My message and my preaching were very plain. . . . But the Holy Spirit was powerful among you.

1 Thessalonians 1:5
When we brought you the Good News . . . the Holy Spirit gave you full assurance that what we said was true.

••• Go ahead and speak, and the Holy Spirit will work in people's heart and mind.

1 Thessalonians 2:4
Our purpose is to please God, not people. He is the one who examines the motives of our hearts.

••• Focus on pleasing God rather than on pleasing people.

What should I do when people aren't interested in hearing about Christ?

Acts 17:32-34
When they heard Paul speak of the resurrection of a person who had been dead, some laughed, but others said, "We want to hear more about this later." That ended Paul's discussion with them, but some joined him and became believers.

••• Some people may not be interested or may even be angry when we talk about Jesus, but we don't know whether there are a few who will believe—so we should speak for their sake.

Ezekiel 2:5, 7-8
Whether they listen or not—for remember, they are rebels—at least they will know they have had a prophet among them. . . . You must give them my messages whether they listen or not. But they won't listen, for they are completely rebellious! Son of man, listen to what I say to you. Do not join them in being a rebel. Open your mouth, and eat what I give you.

2 Timothy 4:2
Preach the word of God. Be persistent, whether the time is favorable or not.

Even if attitudes or circumstances are not good, speak out anyway, and tell about Christ's work.

Luke 9:5
If the people of the village won't receive your message when you enter it, shake off its dust from your feet as you leave. It is a sign that you have abandoned that village to its fate.

If, after we have told them the message, they refuse to accept it, find others to tell.

PROMISE FROM GOD:

John 12:26
All those who want to be my disciples must come and follow me, because my servants must be where I am. And if they follow me, the Father will honor them.

Words

What kinds of words should I speak?

Genesis 50:21
He spoke very kindly to them, reassuring them.

Speak kind words to others.

Psalm 50:23
Giving thanks is a sacrifice that truly honors me.

Romans 15:6
All of you can join together with one voice, giving praise and glory to God, the Father of our Lord Jesus Christ.

●●● Speak words of thanks and praise to God.

Ephesians 4:29
Let everything you say be good and helpful, so that your words will be an encouragement to those who hear them.

●●● Use words that build others up.

Proverbs 15:4
Gentle words bring life and health.

Proverbs 25:15
Patience can persuade a prince, and soft speech can crush strong opposition.

●●● Speak to others with gentleness.

1 Peter 3:9
Don't repay evil for evil. Don't retaliate when people say unkind things about you. Instead, pay them back with a blessing. That is what God wants you to do, and he will bless you for it.

●●● Use your words to bless even those who hurt you.

Zechariah 8:16
This is what you must do: Tell the truth to each other. Render verdicts in your courts that are just and that lead to peace.

●●● Speak truthfully.

What kinds of words should I avoid speaking?

Exodus 22:28
Do not blaspheme God or curse anyone who rules over you.

●●● Never curse God or anyone in leadership over you.

Ecclesiastes 10:20
Never make light of the king, even in your thoughts. And don't make fun of a rich man, either. A little bird may tell them what you have said.

••• Don't make fun of those in leadership.

Psalm 34:12-13
Do any of you want to live a life that is long and good? Then watch your tongue! Keep your lips from telling lies!

••• Don't say anything that is deceptive or false.

Proverbs 18:8
What dainty morsels rumors are—but they sink deep into one's heart.

••• Avoid spreading gossip or talking badly about other people.

Proverbs 29:11
A fool gives full vent to anger, but a wise person quietly holds it back.

••• Avoid speaking in the heat of anger; you will usually regret it later.

James 4:11
Don't speak evil against each other, my dear brothers and sisters. If you criticize each other and condemn each other, then you are criticizing and condemning God's law.

••• Avoid criticizing other people.

PROMISE FROM GOD:

Proverbs 10:11
The words of the godly lead to life.

◦◦◦ Work ◦◦◦

What kind of work should I do?

Genesis 3:19
All your life you will sweat to produce food, until your dying day.

Acts 20:34-35
You know that these hands of mine have worked to pay my own way, and I have even supplied the needs of those who were with me. And I have been a constant example of how you can help the poor by working hard.

1 Corinthians 4:12
We have worked wearily with our own hands to earn our living.

Ephesians 4:28
Begin using your hands for honest work, and then give generously to others in need.

1 Timothy 5:8
Those who won't care for their own relatives, especially those living in the same household, have denied what we believe. Such people are worse than unbelievers.

◦◦◦ Plan on doing work that will allow you to give generously to others.

Matthew 25:34-40
The King will say to those on the right, "Come, you who are blessed by my Father, inherit the Kingdom prepared for you from the foundation of the world. For I was hungry, and you fed me. I was thirsty, and you gave me a drink. I was a stranger, and you invited me into your home. I was naked, and you gave me clothing. I was sick, and you cared for me. I was in prison, and you visited me." Then these righteous ones will reply, "Lord, when did we ever see you hungry and feed you? Or

thirsty and give you something to drink? Or a stranger and show you hospitality? Or naked and give you clothing? When did we ever see you sick or in prison, and visit you?" And the King will tell them, "I assure you, when you did it to one of the least of these my brothers and sisters, you were doing it to me!"

••• Whatever you do, work for Christ's kingdom.

Matthew 5:16
Let your good deeds shine out for all to see, so that everyone will praise your heavenly Father.

••• Do work that will cause other people to praise and glorify God.

Proverbs 13:11
Wealth from get-rich-quick schemes quickly disappears; wealth from hard work grows.

••• Honest, hard work is much better than trying to get rich quickly.

Romans 12:8
If your gift is to encourage others, do it! If you have money, share it generously. If God has given you leadership ability, take the responsibility seriously. And if you have a gift for showing kindness to others, do it gladly.

••• Do work that makes use of your gifts and abilities.

How should I work?

Proverbs 22:29
Do you see any truly competent workers? They will serve kings rather than ordinary people.

Ecclesiastes 9:10
Whatever you do, do well.

●●● Do the best work you can.

Proverbs 10:5
A wise youth works hard all summer; a youth who sleeps away the hour of opportunity brings shame.

●●● Work hard!

Ecclesiastes 10:10
Since a dull ax requires great strength, sharpen the blade. That's the value of wisdom; it helps you succeed.

●●● Be smart in how you work.

Romans 12:11
Never be lazy in your work, but serve the Lord enthusiastically.

Ephesians 6:6-7
Work hard, but not just to please your masters when they are watching. As slaves of Christ, do the will of God with all your heart. Work with enthusiasm, as though you were working for the Lord rather than for people.

●●● Work with enthusiasm at whatever you do, keeping in mind that you are serving God, not people.

James 3:13
If you are wise and understand God's ways, live a life of steady goodness so that only good deeds will pour forth. And if you don't brag about the good you do, then you will be truly wise!

●●● Steadily do good work with an attitude of humility instead of continually pointing out your own accomplishments.

Titus 2:9-10
Slaves must obey their masters and do their best to please them. They must not talk back or steal, but they must show them-

selves to be entirely trustworthy and good. Then they will make the teaching about God our Savior attractive in every way.

••• Be trustworthy and faithful in your work.

Colossians 3:17
Whatever you do or say, let it be as a representative of the Lord Jesus, all the while giving thanks through him to God the Father.

••• Your goal should be to work in such a way that you are a good representative of Christ.

PROMISE FROM GOD:

Colossians 3:23-24
Work hard and cheerfully at whatever you do, as though you were working for the Lord rather than for people. . . . The Lord will give you an inheritance as your reward.

••• Worry •••

When does worry become sin?

Matthew 13:22
The thorny ground represents those who hear and accept the Good News, but all too quickly the message is crowded out by the cares of this life.

Colossians 3:2
Let heaven fill your thoughts. Do not think only about things down here on earth.

••• Worry is like thorny plants—both crowd out what is good. Our worry over the concerns of life becomes sin when it prevents the Word of God from taking root in our life.

Why do I worry so much? How can I worry less?

Psalm 55:4
My heart is in anguish.

●●● Fear and anxiety are normal responses to unknown situations.

Exodus 14:13
Moses told the people, "Don't be afraid. Just stand where you are and watch the Lord rescue you."

●●● We fight worry and anxiety by remembering God's promises and trusting him.

Philippians 4:6
Don't worry about anything; instead, pray about everything.

●●● We combat worry by placing our cares in Jesus' hands.

Psalm 62:6
He alone is my rock and my salvation, my fortress where I will not be shaken.

●●● We find relief from fear in God's promise of salvation.

Matthew 6:27
Can all your worries add a single moment to your life?

●●● Remembering that we will spend eternity with God helps us put our worries about today in the proper perspective.

PROMISE FROM GOD:

1 Peter 5:7
Give all your worries and cares to God, for he cares about what happens to you.

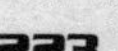

◒◒◒ Worship ◒◒◒

Is worship important?

Exodus 34:8
Moses immediately fell to the ground and worshiped.

2 Kings 17:36
Worship only the Lord, who brought you out of Egypt with such mighty miracles and power. You must worship him and bow before him; offer sacrifices to him alone.

1 Chronicles 16:29
Give to the Lord the glory he deserves! Bring your offering and come to worship him. Worship the Lord in all his holy splendor.

Psalm 145:3
Great is the Lord! He is most worthy of praise! His greatness is beyond discovery!

Isaiah 66:1-2
This is what the Lord says: "Heaven is my throne, and the earth is my footstool. Could you ever build me a temple as good as that? Could you build a dwelling place for me? My hands have made both heaven and earth, and they are mine. I, the Lord, have spoken! I will bless those who have humble and contrite hearts, who tremble at my word."

◒◒◒ Worship is recognizing who God is and who we are in relation to him.

Genesis 35:1
God said to Jacob, "Now move on to Bethel and settle there. Build an altar there to worship me—the God who appeared to you."

◒◒◒ God has told his people to worship him.

Exodus 29:43
I will meet the people of Israel there, and the Tabernacle will be sanctified by my glorious presence.

1 Kings 8:10-11
As the priests came out of the inner sanctuary, a cloud filled the Temple of the Lord. The priests could not continue their work because the glorious presence of the Lord filled the Temple.

2 Chronicles 7:1
When Solomon finished praying, fire flashed down from heaven and burned up the burnt offerings and sacrifices, and the glorious presence of the Lord filled the Temple.

••• God meets with his people in a powerful way when they worship him together.

Deuteronomy 31:11
You must read this law to all the people of Israel when they assemble before the Lord your God at the place he chooses.

Micah 4:2
Come, let us go up to the mountain of the Lord, to the Temple of the God of Israel. There he will teach us his ways, so that we may obey him.

••• Worshipping together gives God's people an important opportunity to hear his Word taught and to learn about God and his ways.

Psalm 5:7
Because of your unfailing love, I can enter your house; with deepest awe I will worship at your Temple.

Psalm 47:7
God is the King over all the earth. Praise him with a psalm!

Psalm 95:1
Come, let us sing to the Lord! Let us give a joyous shout to the rock of our salvation!

Psalm 100:1-4
Shout with joy to the Lord, O earth! Worship the Lord with gladness. Come before him, singing with joy. Acknowledge that the Lord is God! He made us, and we are his. We are his people, the sheep of his pasture. Enter his gates with thanksgiving; go into his courts with praise. Give thanks to him and bless his name.

Isaiah 6:3
In a great chorus they sang, "Holy, holy, holy is the Lord Almighty! The whole earth is filled with his glory!"

Worship is a right response to God's holiness, power, and grace.

Matthew 14:33
Then the disciples worshiped him. "You really are the Son of God!" they exclaimed.

Christ is worthy of our worship.

Revelation 4:9-11
Whenever the living beings give glory and honor and thanks to the one sitting on the throne, the one who lives forever and ever, the twenty-four elders fall down and worship the one who lives forever and ever. And they lay their crowns before the throne and say, "You are worthy, O Lord our God, to receive glory and honor and power. For you created everything, and it is for your pleasure that they exist and were created."

Revelation 5:11-12
I looked again, and I heard the singing of thousands and millions of angels around the throne and the living beings and

the elders. And they sang in a mighty chorus: "The Lamb is worthy—the Lamb who was killed. He is worthy to receive power and riches and wisdom and strength and honor and glory and blessing."

Our worship of God is a taste of what heaven will be like.

How should I worship God?

Genesis 35:2-3
Jacob told everyone in his household, "Destroy your idols, wash yourselves, and put on clean clothing. We are now going to Bethel, where I will build an altar to the God who answered my prayers when I was in distress. He has stayed with me wherever I have gone."

Exodus 20:2-4
I am the Lord your God, who rescued you from slavery in Egypt. Do not worship any other gods besides me. Do not make idols of any kind, whether in the shape of birds or animals or fish.

Deuteronomy 11:16
Do not let your heart turn away from the Lord to worship other gods.

Revelation 22:9
He said, "No, don't worship me. I am a servant of God, just like you and your brothers the prophets, as well as all who obey what is written in this scroll. Worship God!"

We must worship only God!

Exodus 3:5
"Do not come any closer," God told him. "Take off your sandals, for you are standing on holy ground."

●●● When we enter God's presence in worship, we should recognize that we are standing on holy ground.

Psalm 9:11
Sing praises to the Lord who reigns in Jerusalem. Tell the world about his unforgettable deeds.

Psalm 35:18
I will thank you in front of the entire congregation. I will praise you before all the people.

Hebrews 13:15
With Jesus' help, let us continually offer our sacrifice of praise to God by proclaiming the glory of his name.

●●● Our worship should include giving praise and thanks to God for what he has done.

Psalm 30:4
Sing to the Lord, all you godly ones! Praise his holy name.

Psalm 147:1
Praise the Lord! How good it is to sing praises to our God! How delightful and how right!

Ephesians 5:19
You will sing psalms and hymns and spiritual songs among yourselves, making music to the Lord in your hearts.

●●● Singing is an important part of our worship to God.

Psalm 33:2
Praise the Lord with melodies on the lyre; make music for him on the ten-stringed harp.

Psalm 71:22
I will praise you with music on the harp, because you are faithful to your promises, O God. I will sing for you with a lyre, O Holy One of Israel.

Psalm 150:3-5
Praise him with a blast of the trumpet; praise him with the lyre and harp! Praise him with the tambourine and dancing; praise him with stringed instruments and flutes! Praise him with a clash of cymbals; praise him with loud clanging cymbals.

••• Musical instruments play an important role in our worship.

Deuteronomy 31:12-13
Call them all together—men, women, children, and the foreigners living in your towns—so they may listen and learn to fear the Lord your God and carefully obey all the terms of this law. Do this so that your children who have not known these laws will hear them and will learn to fear the Lord your God. Do this as long as you live in the land you are crossing the Jordan to occupy.

2 Chronicles 20:13
All the men of Judah stood before the Lord with their little ones, wives, and children.

••• It is good for everyone in the family to be present together for worship.

1 Chronicles 13:8
David and all Israel were celebrating before God with all their might, singing and playing all kinds of musical instruments—lyres, harps, tambourines, cymbals, and trumpets.

••• Worship can take the form of a joyous celebration with musical instruments.

1 Chronicles 15:16
David also ordered the Levite leaders to appoint a choir of Levites who were singers and musicians to sing joyful songs to the accompaniment of lyres, harps, and cymbals.

••• A choir can be part of worship.

1 Chronicles 16:4
David appointed the following Levites to lead the people in worship before the Ark of the Lord by asking for his blessings and giving thanks and praise to the Lord, the God of Israel.

••• Worship leaders can help guide God's people in worship.

Psalm 95:6
Come, let us worship and bow down. Let us kneel before the Lord our maker.

••• Kneeling and bowing are appropriate during worship.

Hebrews 12:28
Since we are receiving a Kingdom that cannot be destroyed, let us be thankful and please God by worshipping him with holy fear and awe.

••• Holy fear, awe, and thanksgiving should be our attitude in worship.

1 Chronicles 29:10-13
David praised the Lord in the presence of the whole assembly: "O Lord, the God of our ancestor Israel, may you be praised forever and ever! Yours, O Lord, is the greatness, the power, the glory, the victory, and the majesty. Everything in the heavens and on earth is yours, O Lord, and this is your kingdom. We adore you as the one who is over all things. Riches and honor come from you alone, for you rule over everything. Power and might are in your hand, and it is at your discretion that people are made great and given strength. O our God, we thank you and praise your glorious name!"

1 Timothy 2:8
Wherever you assemble, I want men to pray with holy hands lifted up to God, free from anger and controversy.

••• Public prayer is an important part of worship with others.

Amos 5:21-24
I hate all your show and pretense—the hypocrisy of your religious festivals and solemn assemblies. I will not accept your burnt offerings and grain offerings. I won't even notice all your choice peace offerings. Away with your hymns of praise! They are only noise to my ears. I will not listen to your music, no matter how lovely it is. Instead, I want to see a mighty flood of justice, a river of righteous living that will never run dry.

••• Public worship that's hypocritical and unrighteous is worse than useless.

Matthew 2:11
They entered the house where the child and his mother, Mary, were, and they fell down before him and worshiped him. Then they opened their treasure chests and gave him gifts of gold, frankincense, and myrrh.

••• Giving should go along with worship.

Acts 2:46
They worshiped together at the Temple each day, met in homes for the Lord's Supper, and shared their meals with great joy and generosity.

1 Corinthians 11:23-26
This is what the Lord himself said, and I pass it on to you just as I received it. On the night when he was betrayed, the Lord Jesus took a loaf of bread, and when he had given thanks, he broke it and said, "This is my body, which is given for you. Do

this in remembrance of me." In the same way, he took the cup of wine after supper, saying, "This cup is the new covenant between God and you, sealed by the shedding of my blood. Do this in remembrance of me as often as you drink it." For every time you eat this bread and drink this cup, you are announcing the Lord's death until he comes again.

The Lord's Supper is both an act of worship to God and an act of fellowship among believers.

PROMISE FROM GOD:

Psalm 66:4
Everything on earth will worship you; they will sing your praises, shouting your name in glorious songs.

Worth

Of what is God worthy?

2 Samuel 22:4
I will call on the Lord, who is worthy of praise, for he saves me from my enemies.

Psalm 29:1-2
Give honor to the Lord, you angels; give honor to the Lord for his glory and strength. Give honor to the Lord for the glory of his name. Worship the Lord in the splendor of his holiness.

Psalm 33:4
The word of the Lord holds true, and everything he does is worthy of our trust.

Psalm 145:3
Great is the Lord! He is most worthy of praise! His greatness is beyond discovery!

Revelation 4:11
You are worthy, O Lord our God, to receive glory and honor and power. For you created everything, and it is for your pleasure that they exist and were created.

●●● God is worthy of our praise, worship, respect, and trust.

What am I worth—what is my value to God?

Deuteronomy 26:18
The Lord has declared today that you are his people, his own special treasure, just as he promised, and that you must obey all his commands.

Psalm 8:5
You made us only a little lower than God, and you crowned us with glory and honor.

●●● God declares us very valuable to him.

What makes me worthy?

Genesis 1:27
God created people in his own image; God patterned them after himself; male and female he created them.

●●● Each of us is created in God's image. This makes us very valuable.

What does God consider to be worthwhile or valuable?

1 Corinthians 13:13
There are three things that will endure—faith, hope, and love—and the greatest of these is love.

●●● Faith, hope, and love have value that lasts.

Proverbs 4:7
Getting wisdom is the most important thing you can do! And whatever else you do, get good judgment.

Wisdom and good judgment are extremely worthwhile.

Ecclesiastes 7:1
A good reputation is more valuable than the most expensive perfume.

A good reputation has great value.

Proverbs 20:15
Wise speech is rarer and more valuable than gold and rubies.

Wise and helpful words are very valuable.

How can I keep my life focused on things of worth?

Psalm 119:37
Turn my eyes from worthless things, and give me life through your word.

Acts 14:15
We have come to bring you the Good News that you should turn from these worthless things to the living God, who made heaven and earth, the sea, and everything in them.

Acts 20:24
My life is worth nothing unless I use it for doing the work assigned me by the Lord Jesus—the work of telling others the Good News about God's wonderful kindness and love.

2 Corinthians 3:5
It is not that we think we can do anything of lasting value by ourselves. Our only power and success come from God.

Philippians 3:8
Yes, everything else is worthless when compared with the priceless gain of knowing Christ Jesus my Lord. I have discarded everything else, counting it all as garbage, so that I may have Christ.

Philippians 4:8
Dear brothers and sisters, let me say one more thing as I close this letter. Fix your thoughts on what is true and honorable and right. Think about things that are pure and lovely and admirable. Think about things that are excellent and worthy of praise.

When we focus on Christ, the Word of God, heaven, and doing God's work for his kingdom, we can be sure that the focus of our life is worthwhile.

PROMISE FROM GOD:

Psalm 8:5
You made us only a little lower than God, and you crowned us with glory and honor.

Youth

What does God expect from me as a young person?

Proverbs 28:7
Young people who obey the law are wise.

Psalm 119:9
How can a young person stay pure? By obeying your word and following its rules.

God expects you to follow his teachings in the Bible.

Ecclesiastes 12:1
Don't let the excitement of youth cause you to forget your Creator. Honor him in your youth before you grow old and no longer enjoy living.

••• God expects you to honor him.

What if people think less of me because I'm young?

1 Samuel 17:33, 50
[Saul said,] "There is no way you can go against this Philistine. You are only a boy." David triumphed over the Philistine giant with only a stone and sling.

••• Even though David was young, God helped him. God will help you too.

1 Timothy 4:12
Don't let anyone think less of you because you are young. Be an example to all believers in what you teach, in the way you live, in your love, your faith, and your purity.

••• Even though you are young, you can be a godly example to others.

Are there examples of people who served God when they were young?

1 Samuel 2:26
Meanwhile, as young Samuel grew taller, he also continued to gain favor with the Lord and with the people.

2 Chronicles 34:3
During the eighth year of his reign, while he was still young, Josiah began to seek the God of his ancestor David.

Daniel 1:17
God gave these four young men an unusual aptitude for learning the literature and science of the time. And God gave Daniel special ability in understanding the meanings of visions and dreams.

PROMISE FROM GOD:

Jeremiah 3:4
Father, you have been my guide since the days of my youth.

INDEX

Start the trip of a lifetime!

ISBN 1-4143-0043-3

YB™
Young Believer

Collect all 6 books in the Young Believer on Tour series!